PROPERTIUS

CLASSICAL LIFE AND LETTERS

General Editor: HUGH LLOYD-JONES

Regius Professor of Greek in the University of Oxford

Cicero   *D. R. Shackleton Bailey*
Homer   *C. M. Bowra*
Neoplatonism   *R. T. Wallis*
The Presocratics   *Edward Hussey*
Plutarch   *D. A. Russell*
Xenophon   *J. K. Anderson*
Hellenistic Philosophy   *A. A. Long*

Sleeping Maenad. National Museum, Naples (Photo: Mansell-Alinari)

PROPERTIUS

Margaret Hubbard

CHARLES SCRIBNER'S SONS
NEW YORK

Contents

Preface

In a small book designed for the general reader, the complexity of some Propertian problems imposes a dogmatism that needs apology and also silences that I know to be ungrateful. Even in a much larger compass I could not possibly acknowledge all my debts to those who have illuminated the poems for me, and here can only express a general gratitude to anyone who recognises his property. My particular thanks are due to the general editor of the series in which this book appears for his stringent and generous criticism.

I am grateful to Mr. D. A. Russell and the Oxford University Press for allowing me to cite the Longinus passage on page 153; there seemed no point in producing a worse translation of my own.

M.H.

Biographical Note

WE know little of Propertius' life. His own works, a few remarks in Ovid and Pliny, a few inscriptions relating to members of his family, are the only sources. Inscriptions locate at Assisi both some Propertii and Passennus Paullus who, Pliny tells us, was a fellow townsman and perhaps a descendant of the poet, and this is compatible with Propertius' own indications. He himself says that his estate was diminished by confiscations, presumably those of 41/40 B.C., and that he was then still a boy. Ovid, born in 43 B.C., puts Propertius third in the list of elegists, of whom he himself was the fourth, and claims membership of the same social and poetic set; this, and the fact that his first book seems to predate Octavian's triumph of August 29 B.C., suggest a birth date in the early forties. Propertius was therefore a full generation younger than the senior Augustan poets, Virgil (born 70 B.C.), Gallus (70/69 B.C.), Horace (65 B.C.) and their friends. But he began to write young and the period of composition of his first two books coincides with that in which Horace was producing the first collection of the *Odes* (published in 23 B.C.), while Book III came a little later. Book IV cannot be earlier than 16 B.C. and as it contains commissioned poems is probably not much later. In A.D. 2 Ovid implies in the *Remedia Amoris* that Propertius was already dead, but we have no means of knowing how long before.

Propertius in various poems gives chronological indications of the progress of his love affair with Cynthia. These are not easily reconcilable with each other, and attempts to reconcile them are probably misguided. They are no more to be taken literally than the suggestion in the first line of 4.8 that Propertius had dashed off that long and elaborate poem overnight. Such references provide poetic verisimilitude for the moment, not historical data, and the poet was not concerned to make his various poems consistent with each other.

For further discussion of the dates of the books see below pp. 42 ff., and for the nature and importance of Propertius' social status pp. 96 ff.

Introduction

PROPERTIUS' reputation in England, among people who care for Latin poetry, is in some respects a strange one: for almost a hundred years now, he has been acknowledged to be a great poet, but he is also presented as a poet of tormented obscurity, whose defects of expression and of logic, and indeed of Latinity, are allowed to pass because of the depth of passion and psychological insights that they convey or attempt to convey; sometimes indeed these defects are presented as in themselves virtues. Generations of schoolboys have made their first acquaintance with Propertius in Postgate's Macmillan selection, which was first published in 1881 and not only elevated Propertius' reputation but imposed a view of his style that is still current, and still commended, for example in Gordon Williams's *Tradition and Originality in Roman Poetry*, published in 1969. Its starting point is usefully summarised by Postgate himself (p. lxxii):

These contrasts, these extravagancies, these fluctuations and incoherencies, these half-formed or misshapen thoughts, what do they signify? What is the secret of this chaos?

Rather more politely, L. P. Wilkinson said much the same in 1956 (*Fondation Hardt*, vol. 2, p. 219):

. . . he forces his syntax to strange, striking, powerful expressions puzzling at first to the reader. These sudden transitions, the allusiveness, the tortured syntax, are features of our modern poetry . . . Now that readers are accustomed to these features of modern poetry, they are rediscovering the genius of Propertius.

As Wilkinson says, this verdict on Propertian style presents us with a poet we find it easy to be interested in; yet one may reasonably conjecture that it would have dismayed Propertius himself.

If we look at the judgements passed on the poet in antiquity, we find a very different picture, and before we assent to modern opinion, it is worth listening to what the ancients have to say about Propertius. The first of them is Ovid, for whom he is *tener*, sensitive and tender, and *blandus* or *blandi oris*, an expression suggesting an insinuating softness of style rather than the abrupt rigour more recently attributed to him. For Martial he is *facundus*, humorously eloquent. These are poets, and poets not unsympathetic to Propertius. The greatest of Roman critics also passed a crucial judgement on the four Roman elegists. Unfortunately literary historians are in the habit of quoting this judgement phrase by phrase, as they come to each of the poets concerned, and this has led people to suppose that Quintilian said nothing of Propertius except that there were people who preferred him to Tibullus; these nameless people can then be congratulated on their taste in finding in Propertius the qualities we admire today. In fact Quintilian says more about Propertius than is commonly supposed (*Inst.* 10.1.93):

We challenge the Greeks in elegy too. Here the most polished and choice writer is, I think, Tibullus; others prefer Propertius. Ovid is less pruned than either and Gallus harsher.

The passage is a closely knit whole; the two adjectives used of Tibullus are *tersus* and *elegans*, the first referring to smoothness of finish, the opposite of the 'harshness' attributed to Gallus, the second to a choice discretion in style and thought, the reverse of the rampant luxuriance attributed to Ovid. The description is usually admitted to characterise admirably the style of Tibullus; it seems to escape remark that Quintilian regards it as equally apt to Propertius. His quarrel with the anonymous persons is not about what qualities to attribute to either author, but merely about which of them has more of the same qualities. Neither has the luxuriance of Ovid or the harshness of Gallus; both are polished and choice. The verdict was echoed by the younger Pliny when he spoke of the poetry of Passennus Paullus, who claimed descent from Propertius (*Epist.* 9.22.2):

If you take up his elegies, you will read a work polished, tender and agreeably amusing (*tersum, molle, iucundum*), one absolutely written in Propertius' family.

As one would expect from a man both so well educated and so conventional, there is nothing either ill-informed or eccentric about this: Pliny's judgement of Propertius is in line with the best critical opinion of his day.

Ancient criticism knows no dissent from this verdict; it valued in Propertius not an obscure master of the passions, but a poet of finish, grace and charm. Modern critics are less perturbed by this than they should be, and are content, presumably, to acquiesce in Postgate's strictures on the deficiencies of ancient critical thinking and terminology. But though ancient criticism is no doubt short of words for some of the qualities the moderns attribute to Propertius, its terminology for the description of style is elaborate and exact; it is perfectly capable of analysing a harsh abruptness and lightning effectiveness of style, and it certainly does not lack terms for the censure of obscurity. It does not use such terms of Propertius, and those it does use imply the reverse; to reject or neglect this verdict is foolhardy in the extreme.

One gloomy consequence follows and many good scholars have, however reluctantly, brought themselves to accept it:[1] the manuscript tradition of Propertius is much worse than that of most Latin poets. As it presents us with a difficult poet whose words can sometimes hardly be forced into sense, its text is not the one known to the ancient world. In view of what we know of the transmission of the text this is likely enough. A Latin text is best preserved to us if we have a manuscript of late antiquity, of the fourth or fifth century A.D., and also a rich ancient commentary summarising scholarly work that began within or soon after the author's own lifetime; of the Latin poets, Virgil and Terence are in this happy state, and Plautus has an ancient manuscript, though no commentary. One would settle next for several

---

[1] Notably the greatest of all scholars to concern themselves with the poet, Scaliger and Housman; Postgate himself presented a very different Propertius in his later dealings with him. But those dealings are embodied in articles and in the rather repellent pages of the *Corpus Poetarum Latinorum*, not in the attractive ones of the *Select Poems*.

Carolingian manuscripts of the ninth or tenth centuries: these we have for Horace and Juvenal (plus ancient commentaries), for Lucretius and parts of Ovid (without commentaries). Propertius' manuscripts belong to a later period; one, and the better one, is a manuscript of about A.D. 1200 probably written near Metz, while the other, now defective but the parent of a numerous progeny, is about a century younger and is most likely the product of the literary tastes of the thirteenth-century school of Chartres. The latter was copied for Petrarch and its text was known to Italians of the later fourteenth century. It seems unfortunately to have displaced what might well have been a superior tradition, that known to the pre-Petrarchan scholars of Padua, who had some good manuscripts derived from the Cathedral library of Verona or from the Abbey of Pomposa on the Adriatic coast. The older manuscript extant, now the Neapolitanus, was brought to Italy, perhaps by Poggio Bracciolini, soon after 1420, and then a composite class was rapidly formed, correcting some of the errors of the Petrarchan family by conjecture and by collation with the Neapolitanus.

A tradition which like that of the Petrarchan manuscripts comes to us *via* people of literary tastes and information is likely to have much against it, as people of literary tastes and information are unfortunately less good transcribers of manuscripts than servile hacks; they will think and they will tinker and try to improve a corrupt text. If we compare the Petrarchan manuscripts with the Neapolitanus we can see how far the process of depravation can go even within a century or so. This much is visible, but it is probably only the tip of the iceberg. Against an interpolated tradition our best remedy is access to an ancient scholarly tradition such as we have for Virgil, Terence, Horace and Juvenal; such a tradition, however, is attached only to the authors read in schools. For obvious reasons the love poets were not protected in this way, and it seems unhappily likely that at every stage they were preserved and disseminated by people with a taste for poetry and some knowledge of it; not being read in schools, they missed both the acumen of the professional scholars and the faithful unthinkingness of the book trade, and were undefended against the assaults of the amateurs. There is much to indicate that the Neapolitanus itself descends from an already doctored text. Its own scribes have a reassuring appearance of the stupidity and ignorance that lead to honesty; but the text they were copying was already interpolated as well as corrupt. The upshot is that of the major Latin poets only Catullus has a text later and worse attested than that of Propertius.

It is natural to hope that one can know what an ancient poet said, and editors are understandably reluctant to admit that in many passages of Propertius this is impossible. They react in two ways. In the case of Propertius, the attempt at conjectural emendation has probably been more vigorous and persistent than in any other ancient author. Sometimes a lucky shot or penetrating insight leads to a result that convinces, if not everybody, at least the sanguine and judicious; but for every imposing conjecture there are a dozen passages where the transmitted text is indubitably corrupt and where editorial ingenuity has produced six solutions all equally credible and therefore equally inconclusive. A course more damaging to the poet's reputation is taken by those who accept as much as they possibly can of what the manuscripts contain. Part certainly of Propertius' reputation for obscurity has come from his editors' desperate attempts to defend the indefensible by torturing nonsense into a kind of sense and then claiming that in this writer, though not in most writers, the result is tolerable. Housman in a memorable jibe commented: 'Another of those "Propertian peculiarities" which are peculiar not to Propertius but to those authors whose Mss are late and corrupt'; but even editors liberal in admitting particular conjectures have sometimes been shy of confessing that in innumerable instances a wretched tradition has made it difficult for us to be sure what to do. No doubt Propertius was more like, say, Ovid than his manuscripts suggest; but how much more like? Conjectural emendation runs the risk of correcting the poet, conservative criticism the risk of attributing to him the imbecilities of his copyists. Editors, conventional and unconventional, have sought some 'objective' talisman to keep them safe as they try to discover what the author said and what he meant by it, and to free them from the burden of making a judgement in every case of difficulty. There is no such talisman, and those who concern themselves with Propertius are driven to rely on their own taste and discretion, a situation not unexhilarating to those who have the nerve for it.

One more cheerful aspect of the situation may be mentioned. The belief that Propertius is difficult has sometimes led to a self-hypnotised attribution of difficulty to passages that are in fact open, easy and perfectly transmitted. This is where the judgement of the ancient critics can help. If one substitutes the expectation of a graceful and witty Propertius for that of passion's powerful tormented victim, a passage censured for illogicality or obscurity often turns out to contain a witty turn or an unexpected joke. Certainly some Propertian 'difficulties' stem from the poet's belief, obviously justified in antiquity, that his readers would recognise a point of wit or an ironical jest, or for that matter an ironical stance. In this sense the 'allusiveness' and the 'sudden transitions' that Wilkinson speaks of (above, p. 1) really do exist, and one has to watch out for them, though not in Propertius only. The Latin poets nearest to him in this respect are probably Juvenal and Lucan: all three of them work within a rhetorical and poetical tradition that leads the reader to expect that b will follow a; all three of them exploit this fact and aim at the surprise of paradox, where the cultivated reader is expected to savour the collocation of a and not-b. This is a poetry of wit, in a sense more familiar to the seventeenth and eighteenth centuries than to our own. The formidable economy of Horace more austerely deploys the same armoury (often more cryptically too, though much less is made of that than in Propertius' case; Horace is reputed to be an intelligible author); Ovid's fancy elaborates a narrative or dramatic background to give context to similar paradoxes. Juvenal, Lucan and Propertius operate differently: in all of them one feels the lack of the sardonic voice of the reciter mocking the hearer's deluded expectation. Of course there are differences among them: most notably Propertius displays the conscious charm of one who ruefully turns the joke on himself; the reader's expectations about love poetry are disappointed, but so are the poet's expectations about love, and this produces an amiable intimacy between them.

The highest wit of poetry, according to Dr. Johnson, is that 'which is at once natural and new, that which, though not obvious, is, upon its first production, acknowledged to be just ... that which he that never found it wonders how he missed'. Aristotle had said the same in the *Rhetoric* (1412^{a}19 ff.):

Most witty expressions depend not only on metaphor but on rousing a false expectation, as that makes it obvious that one has learned something because of the contrariety, and our soul seems to say 'How true, and I missed it'.

Three centuries intervened between Aristotle and Propertius, centuries in which the universal rhetorical education was formalised and standardised and a new poetry developed, with sapient variation on its predecessors as a principal tool. Though Cicero and Virgil managed it, it was harder for Romans of the first century to rise to the level of 'How true, and I missed it'. The wit of Propertius, perhaps hardly even ambitious for so high an ideal, operates with false expectations that are given, not false expectations that it itself creates. Its suggestions are most often interrogative ('Everyone says *b*, but what if not-*b*?' or sometimes 'Everyone *says b*, but what if really *b*?'); it depends for its effect on a shared background of assumptions and a common culture, and it works by challenging those assumptions. Given this *modus operandi*, there is less reason to be surprised that it has frequently proved elusive.

CHAPTER ONE

The Monobiblos

IT is reasonable to assume of any genre of Latin poetry that it had a Greek original that it formally resembled, however much it might differ in content: this relation exists between Virgil's *Eclogues* and Theocritus' *Idylls*, his *Aeneid* and the poems of Homer, Horace's *Odes* and archaic Greek lyric, the comedies of Plautus and Terence and those of Menander. There are two exceptions to this general picture, satire, of which the Romans claimed the invention, and elegy, where for a complex of reasons they did not realise their own originality. These two genres, though of course they contained much that was derivative from Greek literature and could not have come into existence except for its impulse, nevertheless have no formal equivalent in Greek.

Of course the Greeks wrote poems in elegiac couplets; in early times, from about 700 B.C., the couplet was used for a variety of topics, military exhortation, moralising reflexion, the expression of political and polemical attitudes, of grief, of love, and a host of other subjects. No particular shape or extension was sought; anything from the single couplet up was an acceptable unit of length. The elegiac poet was a reciter or singer, often over the dinner tables, and his limit was what the subject demanded or his audience of the moment would accept. Most of these early elegists are not preserved *in extenso*, but there seems no reason to doubt that if they had been their works would have resembled the extant book of Theognis, some 1,200 lines made up of poems long and short, which though often separable are not separated, formally a shambling monster. This older elegy was bound to retreat in face of the development of prose as the proper medium for dealing with much of its subject matter; by the end of the fifth century it was in decay.

At least two new elegiac forms emerged in consequence, one an innovation, narrative elegy, the other a development of previously existing elements, epigram.[1] The first poet of narrative elegy was Antimachus of Colophon, early in the fourth century; to console himself for the death of his wife Lyde he retold, in a poem called by her name, a series of mythological stories, though we cannot tell whether the themes of these stories had any relevance to Lyde's death, whether, that is, the alleged precipitating factor was exploited as a poetically unifying one. The poem was a long one and severely criticised by Callimachus. The *longueurs* were no doubt largely due to Antimachus' style; Aristotle already complained in the *Rhetoric* (1408^a1 ff.) of his habit of characterising things by negative epithets, that is, stating qualities that a given thing did not have (as he pointed out, such a description need have no end to it). But the *Lyde*, however tedious, was formally innovatory and turned elegy into a path that Callimachus himself was to tread when, in a much more chastened style, he wrote the *Aetia*, a collection of stories explaining the origin of various existing practices and rites.

Other poets, it has been supposed, followed Antimachus' model still more closely. Callimachus' older contemporary Philetas has been thought to have written a *Bittis* which was, like the *Lyde*, called after his wife and might have had a similar purpose; but evidence even for the existence of the poem, not to mention its purpose, is tenuous. At a later date Parthenius of Nicaea wrote an elegiac lament for his wife Arete, and an encomium on her in three books. A finally identified fragment of the former is, however, purely personal in tone, not narrative, and the supposed analogy with Antimachus' *Lyde* seems shaky. Nevertheless, we can hardly doubt that on the model of Callimachus if not of Antimachus Parthenius did practise the narrative mode in elegy, and he is important for us, since he settled in Rome and is linked with the

[1] From early times the elegiac distich or quatrain established itself as the principal, though not the sole, medium for epitaphs and dedicatory epigrams, poems, that is, meant to be carved or written on objects. In Theognis we also find brief developments of a theme, complete in two or four lines, which are not, in this technical sense, epigrams, but have something in common with the later, non-epigraphic epigrams. Hellenistic epigram continues and develops both these lines, and also adds much that is new.

first of the four Roman elegists, C. Cornelius Gallus. An old-fashioned figure, more learned than the contemporary run of Greek poets like Cicero's Archias, he turned the attention of the Romans back to the grander and more difficult models offered by Hellenistic elegy, and may have done much to save Augustan poetry from the trivialities of contemporary epigram.

Parthenius' poetry is almost totally lost, and his only extant work is dedicated to Gallus. This is a little prose book *On Sufferings in Love*, a collection of romantic stories from poetic and fictional sources which, he says, he put together so that Gallus could use them to ornament either epic or elegy. It seems likely enough that Gallus did so, and thus anticipated Propertius in using mythical tales, often *recherché*, to illuminate and highlight the situations, supposed contemporary, that he presented in his love poetry. Indeed even before Gallus we can see something similar in Catullus (who must have known Parthenius through his friend and fellow poet C. Helvius Cinna), when in 68B he uses the love of Laodamia for her husband Protesilaus as an analogy for his own love for Lesbia.

Narrative elegy was thus important to the Roman elegists as a treasure house of *exempla*. It could also be more audaciously used, as Propertius did in 1.18 (and probably Gallus before him); in this elegy the poet does not compare himself with a mythical hero, but represents himself in the same situation. When Propertius seeks out the solitude of the woods, laments his mistress's cruelty and carves her name on trees, he is a modern embodiment of Callimachus' Acontius in the *Aetia*; here narrative elegy is being plundered not for analogies but for fictional situations. More important still, the Roman poets could propose not merely the use of Callimachean themes, but the imitation of his great poem. Catullus had already translated one section of it, *Berenice's Lock*, and Propertius' fourth book contains some fragments of a Roman *Aetia*; Ovid's half-finished *Fasti* continued the ambitious attempt, organising the heterogeneous material on a novel and felicitous principle. More significant than all these, at least and particularly, so far as our knowledge goes, for Propertius, was the influence of the style of Callimachus, that novel amalgam of the highfalutin and the deflating colloquial, where every word had to be approached with circumspection and probed for the information that it and its connotations alone could give of the author's intention, a style most carefully pondered and therefore, in Yeats's sense, 'nonchalant'.

For all these reasons, Roman elegy would have been very different if Greek narrative elegy had not existed. Nevertheless they are formally quite distinct, and until the *Fasti* we have no Roman poem whose structure resembles that of narrative elegy.

Still nearer parallels to Roman elegy are provided by Hellenistic epigram, which shared with it much of its subject matter and which similarly proposed to its poets as a prime task the rehandling, modernising, giving a new turn of wit to a tralatician theme. Many of the techniques deployed by elegy are already present in epigram, the argumentative tone, dramatic setting, developing situation. What principally distinguishes the two genres is scale, which can be quite brutally and numerically expressed: an epigram rarely rises above ten lines, an elegy rarely sinks below twenty. The transition between the two genres can be seen in the poetry of Catullus, whom it is reasonable to reckon the inventor of Roman elegy. Most of the poems in the third part of his book are indubitably epigrams; but some could take their place in any book of elegies, the two epistolary poems 65 and 68A, the subtle and complicated expression of gratitude to Allius 68B, the brooding 76, more like its successors than any other single poem. In all these the refusal to take a single idea and develop it within the neatest possible compass, the search for greater richness and elaboration of a theme, create a new kind of poem that is, nevertheless, a natural development of the epigram.

Catullus' successor was C. Cornelius Gallus, Virgil's contemporary and friend. He wrote four books of *Amores*, addressed like Catullus' love poems to a real person, the actress Cytheris to whom he gave the pseudonym Lycoris, associated, like Delia and Cynthia, with the cult of Apollo. Only one line of his poetry survives, but Virgil's tribute in the tenth eclogue makes it possible to guess at some of the themes he used. It looks as though he lamented the departure of his mistress to a campaign in the frozen north in terms like those Propertius uses in 1.8 of Cynthia's projected journey to Illyria, and that like Propertius in 1.18 he used the Callimachean theme of carving his mistress's name on trees. The coincidence between Gallus and Propertius is useful as a proof, if we needed it, that elegy, like epigram, aimed to give some of its pleasure by rehandling old themes in a new way. What we cannot estimate is the extent to which Gallus anticipated Propertius in the formal development of elegy, though we cannot doubt that he, like Catullus before him, took much of his material from Greek epigram. But it is only in Propertius that we can at last see the means by which an epigrammatic theme, taken as the starting point of a series of reflexions, is used as the germ of a poem quite different from itself.

The techniques of transformation can be seen at once in the first and third poems of the first book (other examples will come up for consideration later in this chapter). For these two poems we have actual parallels in earlier or later Greek epigram, and so can display the very different techniques that Propertius has used to elaborate and develop epigrammatic themes.

The argument from late epigram might seem to need a moment's defence. When Propertius imitates an extant epigram written before his time that, it might be said, is fair enough, but what justifies the inference that a Greek epigram of, say, the sixth century A.D. is indebted to a lost Hellenistic original rather than to Propertius himself? It must be admitted that nothing justifies it as a blanket assumption; some Greeks of late antiquity clearly knew more Latin than we used to think. But the assumption of a lost original remains the more likely when a late Greek author gives us something ordinary where a Roman poet gives us something novel, or something flat where a Roman poet gives us something rich and remarkable; it would be attributing too much perversity even to Greek epigrammatists of late antiquity to assume that they habitually reduced the novel and the rich to banality whenever they took a trait or a theme from a Roman poet. An example from Horace may serve to illustrate the point about novelty. Several Hellenistic poems on the coming of spring conclude with an exhortation to sacrifice a fish to Priapus; for Priapus Horace in *Odes* 1.4 substitutes the figure of Faunus, more meaningful for him, and he suggests alternative sacrifices to him, either a lamb or a kid. When in late epigrams by Theaetetus and Agathias we find Priapus offered a choice of fish, it is not reasonable to assume that they borrowed from Horace only the detail of alternative offerings and left out everything else that was novel in his treatment; instead we infer that alternative offerings to Priapus were found in a Hellenistic original. Similarly, it seems not reasonable to assume that the tedious aridity of Paulus Silentiarius' epigram (below, p. 20) takes its start from the rich texture of Propertius 1.3; once more we infer that the situation it describes (hinted at but not identical with that in Propertius' poem, and much less subtle and complex) was described in a Hellenistic epigram.

The first elegy of the book is a dedicatory poem to Propertius' friend and contemporary Volcacius Tullus (below, p. 24); its opening section is derived from Meleager's elegant celebration of his subjection to the youth Myiscus (*Anth. P.* 12.101, Gow–Page *ciii*):

I was unwounded by Desires, but Myiscus shot me in the heart with his eyes, and cried, 'I have caught the braggart. That supercilious sneer that imperious philosophy gave, look, I am trampling on it.' Just breathing, I replied, 'Dear lad, why all this surprise? Zeus himself was hauled down from Olympus by Love.'

For the six lines of Meleager Propertius gives us 38 and a naturally more complicated structure:

> Cynthia prima suis miserum me cepit ocellis,
>   contactum nullis ante cupidinibus.
> tum mihi constantis deiecit lumina fastus
>   et caput impositis pressit Amor pedibus,
> donec me docuit castas odisse puellas   5
>   improbus, et nullo vivere consilio.
> et mihi iam toto furor hic non deficit anno,
>   cum tamen adversos cogor habere deos.

Milanion nullos fugiendo, Tulle, labores
  saevitiam durae contudit Iasidos.   10
nam modo Partheniis amens errabat in antris,
  ibat et hirsutas ille videre feras;
ille etiam Hylaei percussus vulnere rami
  saucius Arcadiis rupibus ingemuit.
ergo velocem potuit domuisse puellam;   15
  tantum in amore preces et bene facta valent.

In me tardus Amor non ullas cogitat artis,
  nec meminit notas, ut prius, ire vias.

At vos, deductae quibus est fallacia lunae
  et labor in magicis sacra piare focis,   20
en agedum dominae mentem convertite nostrae,
  et facite illa meo palleat ore magis.
tunc ego crediderim vobis et sidera et amnis
  posse Cytaeines ducere carminibus.

Et vos, qui sero lapsum revocatis, amici,   25
  quaerite non sani pectoris auxilia.
fortiter et ferrum saevos patiemur et ignis,
  sit modo libertas quae velit ira loqui.
ferte per extremas gentis et ferte per undas,
  qua non ulla meum femina norit iter.   30

Vos remanete, quibus facili deus annuit aure,
  sitis et in tuto semper amore pares;
in me nostra Venus noctes exercet amaras,
  et nullo vacuus tempore defit Amor.
hoc, moneo, vitate malum; sua quemque moretur   35
  cura, neque assueto mutet amore locum.
quodsi quis monitis tardas adverterit auris,
  heu referet quanto verba dolore meo!

1–8. Cynthia was the first whose eyes captured me, poor wretch, uninfected before by any desires. Then I had to lower my gaze with its steady hauteur and Love trampled on my head, until he relentlessly taught me to hate chaste girls and live by unreason. And for a whole year now this madness does not leave me, though I am forced to find the gods hostile.

9–16. Milanion, Tullus, by not shirking any dangers blunted the cruelty of Iasus' hard-hearted daughter. For sometimes he wandered, out of his mind, in the Parthenian glens, and went to look upon shaggy wild beasts; again he was struck by Hylaeus' club and, wounded, sobbed among Arcadia's crags. So he was able to tame the swift-foot girl; so great is the power of prayer and services in love.

17–18. In my case Love is slow and quite uninventive and does not remember to tread the well-known path as of old.

19–24. But you who have the fraudulent trick of pulling down the moon and whose task is to perform expiatory rites on magic hearths, come on, change my mistress's mind and make her paler than my countenance. Then I should believe your claim to be able to attract the stars and streams with Medea's spells.

25–30. And you, who try too late to call me back from my fall, my friends, look for cures for my insanity. I will bravely put up with steel and cruel fire, if only I can have the freedom to say what my anger wants to say. Take me among the tribes at the world's end, take me over the sea, where no woman can know my route.

31–8. You stay behind, you whom the god has heard and nodded to, and be well-matched in a love unassailed for ever. Against me our goddess uses the weapon of nights of bitterness and Love is never idle, never absent. Avoid this pain, I warn you; let each man persist in what engages *him*, and not change his ground from a love he is used to. Anyone slow to attend to my warnings will repeat my words, alas, with what deep pain!

The differences between elegy and epigram, Latin and Greek, show plainly enough. Discussion of one crucial difference from Meleager, the substitution of 'Cynthia was the first . . .' for 'I was unwounded . . .', may for the moment be postponed (below, pp. 19 f.). The others, though significant, have a more limited importance. For the hackneyed and merely pictorial image of the arrows of love, Propertius gives us the more meaningful one of love as a disease, a madness (*miserum*, *contactum*, *furor* all render this, and the image is continued later in the poem). For the vaunt of Myiscus he substitutes a more terrible subjection to Amor himself. Neither of these ideas is original, and the second indeed probably comes here from elsewhere in Meleager (*Anth. P.* 12.48, Gow–Page *xvi*); but they make the picture denser at this point.

The crucial thing, of course, is that this point is only a beginning, and that the basic theme is richly elaborated as the poem
proceeds. Instead of Meleager, Myiscus and a reminiscence of the
amours of Zeus, elegy presents us with a pair of lovers in an
intellectual and social context, defined by contrasts real and ideal,
assailable by classes of people imagined or actual. The first
contrast sets them off against the ideal world of legend, in which
Milanion's faithful service wins even the chaste huntress Atalanta.
Cynthia was not specially like Atalanta, whose name is left to be
guessed (it is enough that she was cruel and hard-hearted, though
the informed reader may get an extra savour from being reminded
that she was the daughter of Iasus and swift of foot); Milanion,
contrary to legend, is given some traits appropriate to Propertius
(panic at the sight of wild beasts, for instance). As so often, it does
not really matter who they were; any truth about them that is
relevant is given in the poem. Propertius is not always so kind;
and one real difficulty in interpreting him is to determine on each
occasion whether it matters that *this* mythological analogy is used,
so that the poem is genuinely allusive and dependent on something outside itself for its understanding, or whether we are
instantly told all that we need to know.[1] Here certainly all that is
important is the character of the mythical lovers, the idyllic
Arcadian landscape in which their loves are set, and Milanion's
success. The picture is developed in the same number of lines as
Propertius' initial description of his own desperate state. It is
followed by a terse couplet, the central statement of the poem,
that brings us back to Propertius. In his case there is something
wrong with Love: the god is slow, lacking in ingenuity, too
stupid even to remember the well-trodden paths of success
exemplified in the story of Milanion.

In desperation the poet turns for help to two further groups.
The first is abundantly met in literature (though in real life as
well), the witches of aphrodisiac and antaphrodisiac magic. They
claim to pull down the moon; they might set about changing
Cynthia's mind if they want credence for their powers. The
section is conventional and frivolous; the witches are brought in

[1] For an instance where the former seems to be the case see below, pp. 53 f.

only to be derided and dismissed, and one might suspect that their introduction at all is due partly to a notion of what are acceptable erotic commonplaces and partly to a desire for formal balance with the second group appealed to. These are the *amici* who try to recall the young man from his lunacy; in his *envoi* to love and love-poetry (3.24, below, p. 92) Propertius recalls this passage and characterises these *amici* more fully. They are *patrii amici*, his father's friends, people who stand in a relation to him like that of Cicero to the young Caelius or the scandalous Curio (Cic. *Cael.* 9, *Phil.* 2.45 f.), Roman and actual, real deterrents to a young man squandering the family estate on illicit love affairs. But now they have a hopeless case, who professes his readiness to submit to any cure for madness, to surgery, cautery or foreign travel, but warns them before he starts that it is too late. The hint of even brutal actuality takes us a long way from Meleager.

In a last contrast Propertius sets himself against other happy lovers, not now in mythology but in the real world. They need not seek for a cure abroad, and he both wishes them equality in love and enjoins constancy on them. The area of ideas is still Roman, Propertius' present state being contrasted with the Roman and Catullian ideal of the *aeternum sanctae foedus amicitiae*, love as a continuing relation (Lilja 172 ff.). But the concept is again given an edge, which seems novel here, though it later became an elegiac commonplace: such a love may be the gift of god; more realistic and original is the point that it has the advantages of habit (Lilja 114 f.).

One other feature of the poem deserves notice, its unobtrusive elegance of structure. Some strange things have been written in recent years about the importance of the number of lines to a paragraph in Augustan poetry. In the particular case of Propertius, the eccentric edition of O. L. Richmond, as long ago as 1928, lopped and extended the poems to fit a Procrustean notion of their stanzaic composition, and others have urged that quatrains hold the key to the manifold mysteries of Book II. Still, some formal symmetries were clearly found agreeable, and were indeed necessary to give definition to the potentially inchoate elegy. Certainly in Propertius they are always worth looking for, as they help us grasp the articulation of his thought. Our poem as it stands opens with two sections of 8 lines containing the contrasting pictures of Propertius and Milanion. A single couplet follows, the turning point of the poem. Next come two parallel groups of 6 lines on the witches and the *amici*; a final set of 8 restores the harmony of the beginning, though these 8 have a more antithetic and seesaw structure than the opening lines.

Some editors have found or made a different symmetry. *modo* in 11 lacks the balancing adverb that it elsewhere has in Latin; conjecture might supply one, like the *saepe* of a humanist manuscript in 12. But Housman, observing that in the parallel passage of Ovid (*Ars* 2.185 ff.) Milanion carries Atalanta's hunting nets and does not do so here, suggested that a similar couplet containing the missing *modo* was lost from Propertius' manuscripts. Richmond and Enk took up this suggestion, partly because it gave a more symmetric pattern, $8+12+(6+6)+8$. Yet one could argue that such a pattern is too mechanical and that it is more characteristic of Propertius to look for variation as well as an underlying harmony. In the simpler pattern of 1.2, for instance, two groups of 8 lines surround another 16; but the 16 are divided $6+10$, not $8+8$. Moreover, the suggested pattern seems less organically related to the movement of thought. Again, some editors attach the first couplet of the last section to the address to the *amici*. But, even apart from considerations of symmetry, the reiterated *vos* of 19, 25 and 31 suggests three groups, not two, while if the *amici* are, as Propertius tells us, *patrii amici*, they are very unlikely to be also fortunate lovers. Once more, the possibility of such disputes shows that symmetry too, though it can suggest or support interpretations, provides no talisman to the understanding of Propertius. Mere number counting will get one nowhere; but for all that, there is pleasure to be derived from the supple organisation of a Propertian elegy.

It is time now to consider and clarify an important difference of attitude and emphasis between epigram and elegy, a difference that declares itself in the very first words of Meleager's and Propertius' poems, and that is also illustrated, and most vividly, by the third poem of the book: 'I was unwounded by desires . . .',

'Cynthia was the first . . .'. It is probably not unfair to say that one
can read from end to end of the Greek Anthology and hardly find
a poem where the personality and character of the beloved really
matter. The beloved prompts, forwards or obstructs the thoughts
and desires of the lover, but is not *per se* interesting. Much the
same is true of Greek lyric. From the time of Sappho to the time
of Justinian the eye of the Greek lover is turned with passionate
attentiveness on himself. No doubt occasional exceptions to this
generalisation can be found: in Anacreon notably we do find a
delight in at least the person of the beloved, most vivid when conveyed in the image of a charming and beautiful young animal, a
Thracian filly or a fawn trailing after its mother. Yet even this is
far from the conception that we find in Roman elegy of love's
involving the intrusion, sometimes intolerable, of another and
abrasive human personality. This is one debt Western European
literature owes to Catullus.

This Propertius also gives us, and with some novel twists,
sharply exemplified in the third poem. Philodemus had urged the
moonlight to strike through the lattice and fall on Callistion
(*Anth. P.* 5.123, Gow–Page *ix*), and in the poem of a later
epigrammatist we have a description of a situation no doubt
ultimately derived from New Comedy,[1] an evening visit to a girl,
culminating in rape, which is followed by her tears and reproaches (Paulus Silentiarius, *Anth. P.* 5.275):

Lovely Menecratis lay drowned in evening sleep, her arm curving
round her temple. I took courage and climbed on to the bed; and when
I was to my satisfaction halfway along the path of love, the girl woke
from sleep, and with her white hands tried to pull all the hair from my
head. As she struggled we completed the rest of love's work, and
bursting into tears she said, 'Wretch, now you have done what you
wanted, what I have often refused much gold from you for. You will
go off and at once clasp another girl to your breast; you workmen of
love are insatiate.'

It is perhaps unfair to attribute to an Alexandrian poet the
shabby realism of this, which is not improved by the standard

---

[1] Cf. the exploit of Chaerea in Terence, *Eunuchus* 599 ff.

flavouring of homerising diction. But we can reasonably infer that Propertius found in Hellenistic epigram some such vignette, which he has enriched into one of his most marvellous poems.

The sleeping Cynthia is represented in an attitude like that of Menecratis ('her head propped on unsteady hands'), but the picture is made more vivid and more significant by a series of analogies that probably owe as much to art as to literature (cf. pp. 164 f.), the sleeping Ariadne deserted by Theseus, the sleeping Andromeda after Perseus' rescue, an exhausted Maenad. These lift the scene from the prosaic level to one of idyllic beauty, on which Propertius intrudes drunk and shambling, escorted to the house by realistic link-boys. He thinks of rape, but unlike the lover in Paulus' epigram he also thinks better of it, 'fearing the quarrels prompted by the temper I knew so well'; the line looks forward to the later development of the poem, but for the moment it remains a hint and the mood of the opening lines is recreated as the poet gazes at his mistress, rapt like Argus when startled by the strange transformation of Io. Once more the mythical and artistic image serves to remove the scene from the world of every day. He touches her, watches her, takes her very breathing as an omen, fears that she may have a bad dream, fears that someone (no longer himself) may violate her. So intense an expression of awareness of another person's identity has hardly a parallel in ancient literature and few in modern. If Propertius had stopped here he would have written a poem of great beauty and great originality, hair-raisingly skirting a precipitous edge of sentiment without falling over it.

In fact he gives us something better still. Philodemus' moon is put to a use Philodemus did not think of; as its light comes through the opened window it plays 'the busybody to eyes that would else have been laggard' in sleep. The idyllic vision wakes, and not only wakes but talks, and not only talks but nags. It is about time Propertius turned up, refused, no doubt, by somebody else. Where has he been anyway? If only he suffered as Cynthia suffers. Think of her fidelity, like that of the chaste Lucretia, as she sat spinning her wool, of her more sophisticated charms as she sang to a lyre that might have been Orpheus', of the mildness of her plaints of his inconstancy, of the beauty of the sleep that finally overcame her tears. Menecratis, after all, had some cause to complain. But in Propertius the beloved, in contemplation of whom the lover has been rapt and we with him, awakes at once fully armed and ready to seize and exploit any temporary advantage; and she is left with the last word. This surprise turn, so witty, so profound and so truthful, presents the otherness of lover and beloved in a way that even Catullus does not approach. It also shows the poet in a characteristic posture: the objectivity and self-mockery that wait to entrap the sentimental reader is a principal strength of Propertian elegy.

The first poem thus operates on an epigrammatic theme by setting up a series of contrasts to the original picture and so giving it definition and context. The third remains in the narrative mode of its presumed original, but heightens and enriches its banal subject by using mythological and pictorial suggestion to create an idealised scene that is then undercut by Cynthia's lyrical and passionate reproaches. In the second poem Propertius deploys a different technique again, and it may serve as an example of the playful use of the categories of rhetoric to diversify a topic. The elegy is in fact one of a kind very frequent in him and also in Ovid, an example of persuasive argument that we are to imagine not as sent but as spoken to its recipient; in this kind of poem too we need to keep present to us the fact that there are, as it were, two characters on stage, and that love involves the beloved as well as the lover. Awareness of this makes it easier to see how in this poem too Propertius is undercutting what he formally presents: the elegy starts as a little speech, whose theme is elaborated with an elegant formality that would remind any educated Roman of his elementary exercises in rhetoric, but it turns to mock its own elegance.

The subject, the undesirability of expensive dress and make-up, is one that erotic literature derived from New Comedy, and here, as often in similar poems, Propertius deliberately gives his language a colloquial flavour that reminds us of this genesis and is in piquant contrast with other phrases of a higher stylistic level. The juxtaposition is Callimachean, though not Callimachean only, but it is used for a different and more dramatic effect. The opening phrase establishes the tone of the protesting voice (*Quid iuvat . . .?*, 'What is the point . . .?'), and the thesis is stated in this interrogative form, with variety of illustration and an increasingly depreciatory tone,[1] in the first six lines. The next couplet restates the thesis in negative form ('Such dressing up does no good') and offers a clinching reason ('Love himself goes naked and therefore disapproves'). Two sets of supporting arguments follow, one drawn from the world of nature, one from the example of the ancient heroines. These are *parabolai* (comparisons) and *paradeigmata* (examples), standard forms of enlargement that belong to elementary rhetoric. One can profitably compare the recipe for the development of a *gnōmē* or moral tag in the *Elementary Exercises* of the rhetor Aphthonius (Spengel, *Rhetores Graeci* 2.26 f.). In this exercise one leads off with praise of the author of the tag, then paraphrases it, gives a supporting argument for its correctness and then restates the argument antithetically ('For the poor are subject to such and such, whereas the rich . . .'), proceeds to a *parabole* and a *paradeigma*, adduces something similar in another ancient author, and finishes off with a triumphant Q.E.D. In our poem the alternation of positive and negative statements in the series of *paradeigmata* particularly, and quite intentionally, smells of the schools.

But these rhetorical categories are not being merely used in a tedious way; they are being exploited for purposes not their own. At 25 the poem switches from its scholastic movement to a more lively and personal appeal, once more underlined by a colloquialism (the pleonastic *nunc* in 'I am not now afraid'). The solemn and stylised lecture has not, Propertius asserts, been prompted by fear of rivals but by the reflexion that a girl who pleases one man is as well-dressed as she need be; and Cynthia's manifold charms especially will captivate Propertius throughout his life. The compliments are profuse, but once more cut across

---

[1] This is specially visible in the epithets, which in this poem carry much of the weight of sense. Cynthia's silks and perfume are exotically romantic, from Cos and Antioch on the Orontes, but in 4 the gifts she sets herself off with are 'foreign' (dubious to a Roman ear) and in 5 'bought in the market'.

as the poet adds an entertaining condition: his devotion will be perpetual, provided his lecture is effective. Both lecture and compliments dissolve into laughter.

Other notes are struck in the book, but this amiable gaiety is its predominant tone, echoing from an astonishing richness of theme and subject matter, meant to be heard by a mistress and by understanding friends of equally insolent youth. The variety of techniques deployed is almost as remarkable as the variety of theme. Perhaps no single book of Latin poetry so much gives the impression of triumphant talent joyfully exercising itself and unimpeded. Certainly life and poetry were never to be so easy for Propertius again, and the later ages that made a special favourite of the *Monobiblos Properti* responded to a grace and charm not easily paralleled.

The book is unlike many Augustan collections in being a very private one. The world of politics and public affairs is largely absent (for the exception, see pp. 98 f. below). Apart from Cynthia four people are addressed. Two are poets, still young enough to be later close friends of Ovid, who was now about 14, *dulcia convictus membra . . . mei* (*Trist.* 4.10.47 f.), members of a poetic coterie whom Ovid was to remember affectionately in association with Propertius: Bassus wrote iambic invective, Ponticus mythological epic. The dedicatee of the book, Volcacius Tullus, was of a noble family, now established in Rome for more than a century but Etruscan in origin,[1] a family of social status like that of the Propertii, but one that had followed the different road of the Roman official career, attaining its first consulship in 66 B.C. The *gens* had some literary pretensions: one was a jurist, one, Volcacius Sedigitus, had written wooden *senarii* on the history of Latin poetry, while the Pergamene rhetor Moschus was soon to owe his citizenship to Tullus' uncle. Tullus was about to accompany that

---

[1] We cannot say any more. Syme once inferred that the Volcacii came from Perugia, which would put Tullus very near Propertius' own country; but that seems based on a misinterpretation of 1.22.3, which surely means 'If you know the graveyard of our country at Perugia', not 'If you know the graveyard of your home town at Perugia'. The latter would be an idiotic thing for Propertius to say in the context.

uncle to his governorship of Asia; he was another young man, therefore. His promise was destined not to be fulfilled; the delights of Asia detained him, and the virtuous official rise of the Volcacii Tulli was not prolonged. The fourth friend is more difficult to identify, a Gallus, described as noble and warned that his nobility will not help him in love (1.5.23 f.). If we are to take this literally, and there seems no good reason why we should not, some potential candidates are ruled out because their status was equestrian, Aelius Gallus the father-in-law of a kinsman of Propertius, Cornelius Gallus the poet. Indeed the only thing that at all commends the notion that Propertius' Gallus was the poet is the elaborate and Alexandrian style of one of the poems addressed to him (20); guessing in ignorance one would be inclined to say that in this poem more than any other Propertius reflects the style of his predecessor.[1] However, nothing in a book that speaks so exultantly from insolent youth suggests that we should regard Gallus as belonging to a different generation from Propertius and the rest. A middle-aged gentleman of forty, his poetic career in all probability long behind him, his present concerns military and political, would at any rate be unlike the rest of the circle Propertius is talking from. One would be more inclined to see in Gallus an aristocrat adopted into the family of the Aelii Galli or into that of the kinsman of Propertius killed at Perugia, a member again of the Etruscan gentry, of the same social class as Tullus; like Tullus he gets four poems of the book, while Bassus has to be content with one and Ponticus with two or three (7, 9 and very probably 12).

The four friends are not merely honoured with addresses. In the first half of the book they are exploited to give a social context to and a further clarification of Propertius' love for Cynthia. The series of poems following the opening three that define that relation resume the theme of 1.1.25 ff. and show the love exposed to various assaults. Bassus urges on Propertius that many other girls

---

[1] Embarrassed by the manners of 1.10 some suppose that Propertius cannot have seen the love of Gallus and his mistress, but must have read about it in a book: hence Gallus is the poet. The hypothesis raises more difficulties than it solves. What is the point of promising *vestros reticere dolores* (1.10.13) to a poet who had proclaimed those *dolores* in four books more than ten years before?

have charms (4), Gallus would like Cynthia himself (5), Tullus invites his friend to join him in service in Asia (6), Ponticus contemns the abject aims of the love poet in comparison with his own grand enterprise of a *Thebaid* (7). *Come scoglio,* Propertius rebuffs the diverse attacks: none of the assailants realises the uniqueness of his passion and of his mistress; particularly they fail to be aware of her terrible force. Bassus will find the doors of all the girls he commends closed to him for his offence. Gallus' ambition is ludicrously incautious. Like Lesbia (Catullus 68.70) Cynthia is a divinity, but, unlike Lesbia, no *candida diva*; her lover must be prepared to withstand the lightning (1.5.31 f.):

> *Quare quid possit mea Cynthia desine, Galle,*
> *quaerere; non impune illa rogata venit.*

So stop trying to find out what my Cynthia's power is, Gallus; her advent, when she is invoked, is dangerous.[1]

Tullus is preserved from similar terrors by his virtuous disposition (1.6.21 f.):

> *Nam tua non aetas umquam cessavit amori,*
> *semper at armatae cura fuit patriae.*

Your youth has never been slack for love's sake, always your country in arms has engaged you.

In this case it is Propertius whom Cynthia torments with complaints and threats because his friend is urging him to the active

---

[1] The implication of Cynthia's divinity is often missed; yet *non impune, rogata* and *venit* all suggest it (for the similar use of the Greek *elthein* cf. W. S. Barrett's note on Eur. *Hipp.* 529, p. 259). *venit* has the same implication in the second poem to Gallus (1.10) where his own mistress

> irritata venit quando contemnitur illa
> nec meminit iustas ponere laesa minas.

Her advent is angry since she is contemned, and she has no mind, when wronged, to lay aside justified menaces.

So too of Amor himself in the warning to Ponticus that ends 1.7 '*saepe venit magno faenore tardus Amor*'. The implication of *felix*, 'propitious', in the third poem to Gallus (1.13.35) is the same, and the notion of deity is also present in 1.17 (below, p. 34). Roman poets' deification of their mistresses is discussed in Lilja 186 ff., but not everything observable is there observed.

life, his fortune and destiny that she is co-operating with; they decree his prostration, and his decision cannot be in doubt. The virtuous youth can do nothing for him (1.6.31 ff.):

> *At tu seu mollis qua tendit Ionia, seu qua*
> *Lydia Pactoli tingit arata liquor,*
> *seu pedibus terras seu pontum carpere remis*
> *ibis, et accepti pars eris imperii,*
> *tum tibi si qua mei veniet non immemor hora,*   35
> *vivere me duro sidere certus eris.*

But for you, whether where luxurious Ionia stretches or where Pactolus' water dyes with gold the Lydian ploughlands, whether you mean to march on foot or skim the sea and be, as you will be, part of a welcome rule, then if any hour mindful of me comes to you, be assured I live under a cruel star.

Ponticus however is vulnerable: though he puts on airs now (1.7.3 f.)

> *atque, ita sim felix, primo contendis Homero*
> *(sint modo fata tuis mollia carminibus)*

and vie, god bless us, with the prince of poets, Homer (if only destiny is gentle to your poem),

the time may come when he too will be subjected and learn to value the utility of Propertius' poetry.

Pivoting on the poet's successful dissuasion of Cynthia from her Illyrian project (see below, p. 46),[1] the two final poems of this first half of the book show us a comic reversal: the austere Ponticus and the philandering Gallus are now both caught, each themselves in the grip of a unique passion. The poet is merciful to the previous assailants of his love, and advises them with affectionate care. His expertise in love predates theirs, he is a regular oracle of love, better than the doves of Dodona, made expert by pain and tears (1.9.5 ff.). Cynthia, with a bit of help on the side from Amor, has taught him what to aim at and what to avoid (1.10.19 f.); the anxious physician of love echoes the dry language

---

[1] This poem itself picks up the theme of 1.6; cf. Cairns 150 f.

of technical manuals to guarantee his credentials.[1] The prescription follows: no resistance, no haughty words, no sulky silence either; never refuse a request for a present, never promise and fail to perform;[2] total subjection, total concentration on the beloved alone secure success (1.10.29 f.):

> *Is poterit felix una remanere puella,*
> *qui numquam vacuo pectore liber erit.*

The man to win lasting felicity in one mistress is he whose heart is never unengaged, who is never free.

A ring has been agreeably completed: the incurable madman of love whom the first poem shows us has persuaded himself he is the physician (1.10.17 f.):

> *Et possum alterius curas sanare recentis,*
> *nec levis in verbis est medicina meis.*

And I can cure another's fresh obsessions, and the healing power in my words has authority.

Those 'words' demand the rejection of every Roman value; only the heart's affections remain, and the poet displays them as much in his tender care for his friends as in his love. The friendship of the obsessed lover has a different quality from that of the *amici* of the first poem: they tried to recall him from the madness of love; he will show his friends how to live with it, how to profit from obsession. Unlike those *amici*, he knows the answers. The portrait of the band of friends is established, a society outrageous and entertaining, one that has its own preoccupations and its own rules. Within this world Propertius' love for Cynthia makes sense.

The second half of the book is much less tightly knit. One motif is recurrent, the exploration of love in absence, but though recurrent it is not dominant. A letter to Cynthia at Baiae (11) establishes it, and it is then developed in two poems, one (12) probably to Ponticus (a more likely addressee certainly than

---

[1] Cf. Aristotle, *Poetics* 1452^{b}28 f. 'What ought one to aim at and beware of in composing plots?'

[2] *verba benigna* in 1.10.24 must surely refer to the lover's generous promises, not to kind remarks from his mistress.

'Rome that knows my guilt'), one to Gallus (13); both poems have something mechanical about them, and there is something mechanical too in their placing, followed as they are by another once more contrasting Propertius with Tullus (14); this placing seems designed to link the two parts of the book, but somehow fails of effect. The poem to Gallus in particular is perfunctory in structure and shows an unwonted slovenliness in execution; we can reasonably complain of a Latin poet who begins three consecutive couplets with *haec* when the first qualifies *poena*, the second refers to a mistress and the third is neuter plural accusative.

Another brilliant tirade to Cynthia both balances 1.8, so continuing for the moment the diptych pattern of the book, and restores the mood of the opening poems, and also their technique. Once more the poem's starting point is an epigram, a clever dramatic vignette of Meleager's (*Anth. P.* 5.184, Gow–Page *lxxii*):

I'm sure of it, you didn't get away with it. Why the gods? I know what you're up to. I'm sure of it. Stop swearing you didn't. I've found out everything. That's what it was, was it, you cheat? 'Alone' again, you sleep 'alone', do you? What impudence! And now, now once more she says it, 'alone'. Didn't that gorgeous Cleon . . . ? And if not he . . . What's the point of threats? Get out, you vile beast of my bed, get out at once. That's silly; I'll be making you a present of what you want. I know you'd like to see him. So stay here as you are, my prisoner.

Propertius gives his poem a more developed dramatic setting: the poet is ill, Cynthia is slow in coming to visit him, when she appears it is obvious that she has spent her time in doing her hair and dressing up. The women's magazines might commend such behaviour, but the poet will have none of that. Like Cynthia herself in 1.3 he seizes at once on the chance to attack. In a torrential storm the reproaches pour out:

> *Saepe ego multa tuae levitatis dura timebam,*
> *   hac tamen excepta, Cynthia, perfidia.*
> *aspice me quanto rapiat fortuna periclo.*
> *   tu tamen in nostro lenta timore venis.*
> *et potes hesternos manibus componere crinis*   5
> *   et longa faciem quaerere desidia,*

nec minus Eois pectus variare lapillis,
ut formosa novo quae parat ire viro

1–8. Often and often I dreaded your cruel frivolity, only not this
treachery, Cynthia. See how great the peril fortune is hurrying me off
in; and yet you, in this terror of mine, are slow to come. And you have
the heart to rearrange your hair, disordered since yesterday, and to sit
about for ever trying to improve your looks, *and* to make your breast
bright with eastern jewels, like a girl preparing to go in beauty to her
bridegroom.

The scornful analogy is sharp-edged. Cynthia has stepped out of
her role; she is not the sort of girl to be a Roman bride. With
startling economy Propertius has given us not merely his particular scene, but its social context. Here again, the glancing
allusion to a different world gives the lovers' moment a density
beyond Meleager.

Cynthia should find her analogies in a quite other area, that of
the beautiful heroines of antiquity whose love endured after
desertion or after death. In that world the boundaries between
mistress and wife are blurred: the poet gives four examples,
divided indifferently between them, but the conjugality of the two
wives is emphasised by repetition (*coniuge, coniugis*).[1] Calypso
makes the transition: deserted by Ulysses she did not do her hair;
in that ideal world, she had other things to think about:

> *At non sic Ithaci digressu mota Calypso*
> *desertis olim fleverat aequoribus:*
> *multos illa dies incomptis maesta capillis*
> *sederat, iniusto multa locuta salo.*
> *et quamvis numquam post haec visura, dolebat*
> *illa tamen, longae conscia laetitiae.*

9–14. But Calypso did not behave so: in turmoil at Ulysses' departure she wept of old by the deserted seas. For many days she sat
lamenting, her hair uncombed, complaining to the injurious waves.
And though she was never to see him again, she felt passionate grief,
aware of their long gladness.

[1] We may note that Propertius apparently invents one of the two; the rest
of the mythographic tradition knows nothing of the motive he attributes to
Alphesiboea.

That is the real point of contrast, after the jest of *incomptis capillis*; in the world of myth there was, in the world created by poetry there might be, a love that does not depend on presence. The motif of love in absence, dealt with *scherzando* in some of the surrounding poems, gets a new dimension that in this book is further investigated in poem 19, and that recurs throughout, with emphases ranging from Propertius' hesitant injunction (2.13.51 f.):

> *Tu tamen amisso non numquam flebis amico;*
> *fas est praeteritos semper amare viros.*

Weep sometimes for your friend though he is lost; it is licit to go on loving lovers gone,

to the dead Cynthia's triumphant claim (4.7.93 f.):

> *Nunc te possideant aliae; mox sola tenebo.*
> *mecum eris, et mixtis ossibus ossa teram.*

For now let others have temporary ownership of you; soon I alone shall hold you; you will be with me, and mingling my bones with yours I shall press them hard.

Such love is a paradox, not to be taken for granted, and in our poem its paradoxical nature is underlined by the unexpected '*And though* she was never to see him again . . .'

The next example adds another detail. Hypsipyle did not merely lament Jason's loss. Once the infection of love for him had struck her down she was insensible to all other passions. Propertius pushes his next two cases to the edge of the terrifying and the absurd (the wives go further than the mistresses): Alphesiboea killed her brothers to avenge her husband, Evadne committed suttee on the pyre of Capaneus. And yet Cynthia refuses to learn from them. By overbalancing into hyperbole the poem recovers its comic poise.

From these highflown and romantic exemplars we revert with a thud to the real world. Like Meleager's girl Cynthia says something, protests her fidelity, we infer. As in Meleager we guess her words only from the poet's retort:

> *Desine iam revocare tuis periuria verbis,*
> *Cynthia, et oblitos parce movere deos.*

25–6. That's enough. Stop recalling your false oaths, Cynthia, and don't stir up the forgetful gods.

Yet at this point where the lovers are most clearly in dialogue, their identity is also most clearly stressed. Cynthia should be wary of the gods for his sake, not her own:

> *Audax a nimium, nostro dolitura periclo,*
> *siquid forte tibi durius inciderit.*

27–8. Ah all too bold, it is at my cost that you will suffer if anything cruel comes upon you.

As for him, the order of nature must be overturned before he ceases to love her, but on one condition:

> *Sis quodcumque voles, non aliena tamen.*
> *tam tibi ne viles isti videantur ocelli,*
> *per quos saepe mihi credita perfidia est.*

32–4. Be whatever you like, only not another's. Do not rate so cheap those eyes of yours, those eyes you have often sworn by and made me trust your treachery.

Between threats and denunciations the poem moves in a comic *crescendo* to its end:

> *Quis ego nunc pereo, similis moniturus amantis,*
> *'O nullis tutum credere blanditiis!'*

41–2. Those eyes now bring me to death and my death will warn lovers like me, 'Oh there are no blandishments it is safe to trust!'

What did Cynthia say next? The structure of the poem invites the question, but leaves us to guess; this time it is Propertius who has the last word. But by the end of this poem we have become aware of something new. The picture of the love of Propertius and Cynthia was developed in the earlier poems, with epigrammatic themes refined by intimations of various worlds they did not fit. That happens here too. But there is also something more, dependent on the fact that these varying poems are part of a book and expand each other. The third and the fifteenth poem, ending as each does at a moment that invites the reader to imaginative continuance, gain point from their association with each other.

In 1.5.2 Propertius had urged Gallus to let him and Cynthia go on in the course they were on, a well-matched pair; whether of oxen or race horses, the image is trite and conventional. By now another image has been substituted, finally defined in 1.15: a well-matched pair, a *par compar*, but of gladiators, whose warfare is sport but can be deadly.

From this high point the book runs out in elegance. None of the poems that follow are bad poems: in grace and agreeableness, variety and ingenuity they provide a bravura display that brings the book to a close in harmony with its beginning. In 1.16 as in 1.8 Propertius plays with a standard form: there he had asked, 'What if a conventional *propempticon* or farewell address were a successful speech of persuasion?' (see below, p. 46); here he asks, 'What is a door's attitude to the lover's serenade?', and agreeably contrasts the door's affronted pompousness with a lover's sentimentality (not his own; the lover in question has a taste for emotional diminutives that Propertius does not share).

A similar play of fancy informs the next two poems, soliloquies of the lover in absence, stormbound on a wild shore or roaming like Callimachus' Acontius in the woods. Here Propertius speaks again in his own person; what, is his question, could a modern lover have to say in these imagined situations? The answer is in some ways surprising: he expostulates with his mistress. Absent or present, it is all the same; the pressure exerted by another personality, the urgent need to lessen it by argument or pleading persist in absence as in presence. The technique is bold, quite different from that of an obviously epistolary poem like 1.11, but it is not novel in Propertius. Even in the sixth century B.C. Solon from the other side of the Aegean had expostulated with Mimnermus (frr. 20 f.), and in a situation more like that of our poems Catullus, taking a hint from Callimachus, had made his Ariadne address her reproaches to the distant Theseus. It is moreover a reasonable inference from the tenth Eclogue that Gallus had lamented to an absent Lycoris. What is probably novel is Propertius' pretence that in the circumstances successful persuasion is possible, and the comic extremity to which he pushes the idea in the first of these two poems. Cynthia does not merely control the poet's thought; she controls the storm that is punishing his attempt to escape. The angry goddess is revealed in startling power, in a power that is indeed startling even in a goddess:

Quin etiam absenti prosunt tibi, Cynthia, venti.

Why, even though you are absent, Cynthia, the winds do you service.[1]

They would not do as much for Aeolus, their own god; the power of ancient deities was in general confined to their immediate neighbourhood. Cowed, the poet begs for cessation; she has overdone things and cannot really want his death. Or can she?[2] Ruefully he contrasts his present situation with an imagined fate if he had stayed obediently in Rome, a bourgeois funeral with all the trimmings, with Cynthia behaving like any conventional and affectionate mortal. The Nereids, tender-hearted girls themselves and like him victims of love, are invoked to restore him to civilised shores. Once more the point of the poem lies in taking literally the sentimentalities of love poetry. What if it were really true that addresses to an absent mistress had some purpose? What if she really were a goddess? The questions suggest the scene in which the conventional pretences can have substance, the lonely halcyons, the squalls, the shore that rejects the poet's prayers and that will soon cover his body with a thin layer of sand, the strand encompassed by unknown woods, the poet looking in vain for the longed-for Tyndarids. The scene is not imagined without the help of conventional forms: the Tyndarids belong to the *propempticon*, Cassiope (3) probably locates the poet on the journey to Greece that is the one most often envisaged in Roman *propemptica*, the prayer to the Nereids is the conventional close to a *propempticon*, but here gets a novel twist because the traveller has to utter it himself. Standard forms thus in some degree determine the direction the poet's fancy takes; but they are no more sufficient to explain the whole poem than a collection of *loci communes* is to

[1] Hostile gods are to be expected in such a context; cf. Cairns 66. Cairns misses the implication here; but if Cynthia were merely a mortal, Propertius would be surprised not that she can control the storm in absence but that she can control it at all.

[2] In 11 I take it that Baehrens's *reposcere* in the sense 'demand as due' is what Propertius wrote.

explain the sinuous argumentation of a Ciceronian speech. Imagination here is not just using a convention but playing with it, and it is the play that gives point and elegance to the poem.

After the Callimachean prettiness of 1.18, 1.19 takes up and pushes further the implications of 1.15. Love enduring after death implies what? Perhaps images familiar from the Greek poets, though given a new application: the poet's shade in the Underworld will austerely reject the advances of the beautiful heroines of antiquity. But other and more surprising images press in too. The loving and beloved poet will be dust or glowing embers (1.19.5 f., 19, 21 f.):

> *Non adeo leviter nostris puer haesit ocellis*
> *ut meus oblito pulvis amore vacet.*

The lad (Love) has not fixed himself in my eyes lightly enough for my dust to forget and be free of love.

> *Quae tu viva mea possis sentire favilla.*

May you live and be aware of all this when I am glowing embers.

> *Quam vereor ne te contempto, Cynthia, busto*
> *abstrahat a nostro pulvere iniquus Amor.*

How afraid I am that unkind Love will make you despise my grave and tear you away from my dust.

The loving and beloved Cynthia when they are reunited will be bones, no more. It is a standard doctrine among Propertian editors that the poet often says 'bones' when he means 'shade' and 'shade' or something similar when he means 'bones'. This is quite false. When Propertius speaks of bones, dust, embers, our attention should be fixed on physical remains; that these can love and be loved is the extreme paradox of love, far outdoing sentimental reunions on the banks of Acheron.

It is not a question of

Can these bones live?

These bones do live and have power; *qua* creatures of power they are not the shades of the Greek underworld but the *manes* of Roman funerary cult, the alarming spirits of the dead, to which

poetry assimilated the Greek shades. The *manes*, like the bones
and ashes of the dead, inhabit the funerary urn; indeed they *are*
the bones and ashes, conceived as still *empsycha*, possessed of
sensation and feeling. Two couplets of Propertius clearly show
his identification of the *manes* with bones and ash (2.13.31 f.,
57 f.):

> *Deinde, ubi suppositus cinerem me fecerit ardor,*
> *accipiat Manis parvula testa meos.*

Then, when the fire underneath has turned me to ash, let a little pot
receive my *manes*.

> *Sed frustra mutos revocabis, Cynthia, Manis.*
> *nam mea qui poterunt ossa minuta loqui?*

But it will do no good to call back my dumb *manes*, Cynthia. For how
will my shattered bones be able to speak?

This is not 'confusion' of bones and *manes*, much less a meta-
phorical use of one word for another, but a clear statement of their
identity. This idea is not in the least peculiar to Propertius; it
finds expression in Virgil, in a writer so prosaic as the younger
Pliny, and in inscriptions.[1] What has perhaps misled us is that,
alongside conventional Greek images, the poet's imagination is
here operating with distinctively Roman ones, characteristically
vague and lacking in plastic form, but not so lacking in plastic
form that we should avert our gaze from the physical contents of
the funerary urn and prefer to think exclusively of the lively
creatures with which Greek fancy populated the realm of Hades.[2]

A graceful bit of Alexandrianism follows, a warning to Gallus
to guard a favourite slave boy called Hylas from the assaults of

---

[1] Cf. F. Cumont, *Afterlife in Roman Paganism*, New York, 1959, pp. 48 ff.;
R. Lattimore, *Themes in Greek and Latin Epitaphs*, Urbana, 1962 (= *Illinois
Studies in Language and Literature*, 28, 1942, 1–2), pp. 91 f.

[2] That it is a preference is curiously underlined by the comment of one editor
on 4.7.94, 'You will be with me, and mingling my bones with yours I will press
them hard': 'Thus the sentence as a whole perhaps is meant to say only that her
shade will hold his in a tight embrace. But the primary meanings of the words
composing it *are hard to escape from*.' Cultivated Englishmen confronted by the
exuberant personality cherished in Italian cemeteries of the present day feel a
similar desire to escape.

the Ausonian nymphs who haunt the watering places of Italy (20);
the warning is reinforced by a lush retelling of the story of the
mythical Hylas, the beloved of Hercules, drowned by the nymphs
who fell in love with him as he was drawing water for the Argonauts. The story was a favourite one, told not only by Apollonius
but by Theocritus (*Idyll* 13), who, like Propertius, treats it as
an *exemplum* for something in contemporary life, and also by
Nicander in the *Heteroeumena*. In Latin it must have featured in
the *Argonautica* of Varro of Atax, and Virgil's reference to it in
the sixth *Eclogue* perhaps suggests that Cornelius Gallus had made
some use of it. Ovid took to heart Virgil's more dismissive
remark in *Georgics* 3.6 'Who has not told of the lad Hylas?', and,
in spite of Nicander, made no place for the legend in the *Meta-
morphoses*; he had in the story of Narcissus a less trite and more
significant instance of metamorphosis into a spring and it is there
that he challenges comparison with our poem.

In dealing with this well-worn topic Propertius deploys a style
quite unlike anything in the rest of the book. Both in rhythm and
in diction it exhibits a mannered preciosity that is the Roman
version of an Alexandrian style, characterised by self-conscious
parade and sapient allusiveness.

> *Hoc pro continuo te, Galle, monemus amore*
> (*id tibi ne vacuo defluat ex animo*).

This is the advice my unbroken affection for you prompts, Gallus (let
it not slip from your mind and leave it empty).

The *sententia* that this highflown couplet introduces is more
commonplace than its prelude leads us to expect:

> *Saepe imprudenti fortuna occurrit amanti.*

If a lover does not take thought, fortune often crosses him.

An attestation follows:

> *Crudelis Minyis dixerit Ascanius.*

Ascanius, cruel to the Minyae, shall say so.

What is this? Who is Ascanius? Not, certainly, the one we know most about, the son of Aeneas; he has nothing to do with the Minyae, the Argonauts. We have the name again in line 16, where the wandering Hercules (called, in a grand epic periphrasis, 'the wandering of Hercules') is said to have wept to 'untamed Ascanius'. The poet tells us no more. We have to go elsewhere to find out that Ascanius is a river.

This kind of enigma belongs to the style of the late Republic, reminding us of the reputation of Cinna's *Zmyrna*. It is true that Propertius is fond of learned allusion; but it is also true that he rarely leaves us, as he does here, in a total fog about what is being said, whether or not we happen to be in possession of some piece of recondite lore. We saw how in the first poem the analogy of Milanion and Atalanta was, as it were, completely cashed out by the description given of their nature and fate. Other cases are a little more opaque, but not much more. For example, Propertius says (1.2.15 ff.):

> *Non sic Leucippis succendit Castora Phoebe,*
> *Pollucem cultu non Hilaira soror;*
> *non, Idae et cupido quondam discordia Phoebo,*
> *Eveni patriis filia litoribus;*
> *nec Phrygium falso traxit candore maritum*
> *avecta externis Hippodamia rotis;*
> *sed facies aderat nullis obnoxia gemmis,*
> *qualis Apelleis est color in tabulis.*

It was not thus that Leucippus' daughter Phoebe fired Castor, not by her dress that her sister Hilaira won Pollux; nor she, once the cause of strife between Idas and desirous Phoebus, Evenus' daughter on the banks of her father's stream; the whiteness by which Hippodamia attracted her Phrygian husband was not false, Hippodamia carried off on foreign wheels; she had a face not spoilt by any gems, brilliant as the colour in Apelles' paintings.

Though our response to this and to many such passages may be enriched by information about the identity of these heroines, and will certainly be enriched if our imagination, like Propertius' own, is stored with the images of them presented by classical painting and sculpture, the intellect has no ground for being perplexed.

Here too we know perfectly well what is being said. More difficult are cases like that of 2.28 (below, pp. 53 f.), where the choice of examples is determined by the line of argument, and one could not, as one could in 1.2 and often elsewhere, substitute another bunch of heroines and make precisely the same statement. But that too is far from the deliberate riddling, intended to mislead the uninitiated, of

Ascanius, cruel to the Minyae, shall say so.

One can note also two rather lengthy developments of pictorial subjects, the assault of the winged sons of Boreas on the boy Hylas and the *ecphrasis* of the scene at the spring; the second is a favourite artistic subject, the first not known in art but illustratable by frequent pictures of the rape of Orithyia by the Boreads' father (below, p. 173). Both are uncharacteristically self-indulgent, the *ecphrasis* of the spring particularly so, with its lonely trees and dewy apples, white lilies and scarlet poppies. Propertius' landscapes do not normally exhibit features so lacking in point. In this book one can contrast the vivid and affectionate detail of the description of Tullus in his park (1.14.1 ff.):

> *Tu licet abiectus Tiberina molliter unda*
> *Lesbia Mentoreo vina bibas opere,*
> *et modo tam celeres mireris currere lintres*
> *et modo tam tardas funibus ire ratis,*
> *et nemus omne satas intendat vertice silvas,*
> *urgetur quantis Caucasus arboribus . . .*

Though you sprawl comfortably by the waves of the Tiber and drink Lesbian wine from a masterpiece of Mentor's, and marvel now that the skiffs speed on so swiftly, now that the barges are dragged so slow, and though the whole wood rear high timbers grown from seed, tall as those giant trees that weigh down the Caucasus . . .

The scene is sharply presented to the eye, but no detail is otiose, conventional or merely pictorial: Tullus' gardens are in the most fashionable spot, his wine is the sweetest, his silver cup an old master, his occupation shows the disengaged interest of a Roman grandee on vacation (compare, for instance, Cic. *Att.* 13.21.3), his wood is planted not native, full grown not the recent mania of a *nouveau riche*. As characteristic is the fully imagined landscape of 1.17, emerging as it does from the poet's rueful deprecation of his fate. For all its elegance, the Hylas poem exhales a marked fragrance of Turkish delight. More than any other poem in the book it suggests pastiche and, very likely, pastiche of the manner of Cornelius Gallus; given this eccentricity, its conspicuous position near the end of the book is something of a puzzle.

It is indeed in a sense the last poem of the book, as the two closely related epigrams that follow make up the *sphragis* or seal that we find at the end of many ancient works, where the poet, in default of a dust jacket, gives us what biographical information about himself he regards as relevant. Of the epigrams one is dramatic, put into the mouth of yet another Gallus dying near Perugia, murdered by unknown hands after escaping through the army of Octavian, while the second tells us that this Gallus was the poet's kinsman and that the part of Umbria nearest to the ruined city was his *patria*. From a poet writing after Actium, the declaration is unexpected and indeed startling, and it brings the book to a troubling close.

CHAPTER TWO

Some Problems of Unity

A CENTRAL difficulty in coming to grips with Propertius is the fact that Book II, though it contains some of his greatest poetry, is also in more considerable confusion than any other part of his work. Some of the trouble is deep-seated in the tradition. The book is 1,362 lines long, far longer than any other collection of similar poems, the nearest parallel in Augustan literature being the 1,004 lines of the third book of Horace's *Odes*. All we know of the Augustan book trade suggests an increasing standardisation of the size of the book, and particularly a tendency to regard 1,000 lines as an upper limit; the other books of Propertius (706, 990, 952) conform to this tendency. Genre is also relevant. From both points of view a book of love poetry 1,362 lines long is a monster.[1] In 2.13.25 Propertius expresses his wish for a funeral escort of three smallish books (*libelli*), and Lachmann reasonably inferred that we have in Book II the remains of two books, one certainly defective, one perhaps complete. He found a proem for the second in 2.10, not implausibly.

Lachmann's theory was produced in 1816 and remained in vogue for a century. Current fashion tends to reject it, but without really countering Lachmann's arguments (the cautious summary in Butler and Barber's introduction is more temperate than most). More recently, Gordon Williams has suggested that the mention of 'three books' could be explained by the simultaneous publication of Books I–III as a cycle on Propertius' love affair with Cynthia; but even apart from the fact that it does not confront the problem of length, this theory involves difficulties. In particular

---

[1] Conservative editors point triumphantly to the fact that there is *a* longer book of Latin poetry, the 1,457 lines of Lucretius V, as though the posthumous work of a didactic philosopher could conceivably be a useful precedent for a live love poet writing twenty-five years later.

3.20 is a late poem, as some linguistic features show, but it has, both on Williams's hypothesis and probably in fact, an early dramatic date. If the earlier books were not already beyond recall, why did Propertius not use an early poem to achieve the effect of immediate contrast with the farewell to Cynthia that Williams argues for? It is also worth noting that the cycle would be recording not just the love affair with Cynthia but the poet's reconciliation with the Augustan *régime*. Nor could one say that this is the accidental result of putting poems of the same period in a single book; those referring to Maecenas and Augustus are too carefully placed for that, and 1.21 in particular would astonish (below, p. 43). Moreover, though Williams's hypothesis depends on the argument that poems became known in literary circles without publication in book form, it fails to explain the fact that it is only in Book III that Propertius shows the influence of Horace's *Odes*, published in 23 B.C., though many of them were written much earlier. Finally, such chronological indications as the poems themselves yield are compatible with the hypothesis of separate publication of the books, and simultaneous publication of a chronologically arranged collection would be more of a novelty than Williams allows: the examples of Catullus, of the *Eclogues*, and of the three books of Horace's *Odes* show a high indifference to date of composition as an ordering principle.

'Sometimes one conjectures right, and sometimes one conjectures wrong.' But it seems necessary at any rate to attempt an outline sketch of Propertius' *biographia literaria* on the basis of such scanty indications as the poems provide, and to try to fit this into the history of Augustan poetry in the twenties, the most dazzling decade of Roman poetry.

Apart from the war at Perugia, long past, the only datable event referred to in Book I is the proconsulship of Tullus' uncle (1.6.19 f.). This is dated by R. Hanslik (*RE* Suppl. 9.1839) to 27/26 B.C., by K. M. T. Atkinson (*Historia* 7, 1958, 312) to 26/25 B.C. Both dates make the chronology of Propertius' *oeuvre* hard to make any sense of. Fortunately inspection reveals that they rest on nothing better than the hypothesis that the *princeps* was, through years of war and revolution, with half the consulars of the thirties hopelessly compromised as ex-Antonians, nevertheless faithfully observing the provisions of the Lex Pompeia of 52 B.C., which enjoined a five-year gap between consulship and pro-consulship: the hypothesis seems hopeful, not to say audacious. Propertius' description of Tullus' task ('to bring back traditional rights to the allies who have forgotten what that is') better suits a date soon after Actium than one when the East had been enjoy-ing the benefits of the *princeps'* rule for four or five years. Mrs. Atkinson points to the grant of *libertas* to Chios in 26 B.C., and the confirmation of the treaty of Mytilene in 25 B.C.; but such things hardly justify a poet in saying that three years after Octavian's triumph over Cleopatra the East was still anarchic. The Propertian commentators therefore seem to have better grounds when they put the proconsulship in 30/29 B.C. or 29/28 B.C.; this would give spring 30 or spring 29 as a *terminus post quem* for Book I. Even at these dates 1.21 is a surprising poem; as a poem first widely published in 26 B.C. it would be still more so, as one, on Williams's hypothesis, first widely published in 22 or 21 B.C., hardly imaginable. The poem does not trouble Mrs. Atkinson as it should, as she seems to assume that the Gallus who died by unknown hands after escaping through Caesar's swords and whose bones were to be found among others scattered on Etruscan mountains is Cornelius Gallus the poet, who died by his own hand in Egypt in 26 B.C. after Augustus had renounced his friendship; but this is implausible.

The further data are these: (1) 2.1 refers to Octavian's triumphs of August 29 B.C.; it is also mockingly countered by Horace in *Odes* 2.12; (2) 2.3 suggests that the interval between the *Mono-biblos* and its successor was a short one; (3) 2.7 apparently refers to an abortive attempt by the *princeps* to introduce moral reforms, most likely early in 28 B.C.; (4) in 2.10 Octavian has become Augustus (January 27 B.C.) and we have references to the sub-mission of India and to Arabia's fear of invasion, both events datable to 26 B.C.; (5) 2.34 refers to the death of Cornelius Gallus; (6) 2.31 has often been taken to allude to the dedication of the Palatine temple to Apollo (October 28 B.C.); but Propertius seems in fact to be talking about the opening of the attached portico, not the temple dedication, and the poem may well be later; (7) many poems in Book III show the influence of Horace's *Odes*, a relation opposite to that between 2.1 and *Odes* 2.12; (8) Book III is later than the death of Marcellus (autumn 23 B.C.), but probably earlier than Augustus' accommodation with Parthia in 20 B.C.

These data would be satisfied by a scheme something like this: Book I mid or late 29 B.C., Book II (first part) 28 or early 27 B.C., Book II (second part) late 26 or 25 B.C., Book III 22 or 21 B.C. Between the date suggested for the first and second parts of our present Book II we can, on the most probable hypothesis, locate the publication of Tibullus' first book, and in the longer gap between II and III the publication of Horace *Odes* I–III, both, I should suggest, significant spurs to Propertius' poetic activity.

Another and more serious difficulty is also presented by the manuscript tradition of Book II, though this time it may not be caused by it. Its nature can best be shown by some brief statistics. The reader of Propertius who takes up a modern edition like Barber's Oxford Classical Text finds himself presented in Book II with 46 poems, ranging from a four-line fragment (an epigram?) to the elaborate 78-line composition of 2.1. If he is surprised by this and investigates what the manuscripts present us with, he will find 32 or 33 poems in the Neapolitanus, and 27 in the Petrarchan tradition (with some slight differences among the manuscripts of this class about what the 27 are). Particularly he will find that towards the end of the book the manuscripts just give up any attempt to distinguish poem from poem: the earliest extant Petrarchan manuscript (F) has a continuous block of text from the beginning of 28 to the end of 32, two later ones from the beginning of 29 to the end of 32; all of them link 33 and 34; the scribe of the Neapolitanus similarly has a continuous block from the end of 31 to the end of 34, though his rubricator provided a break between 32 and 33. Moreover, attention to the numbering of the poems and the remarks in the *apparatus criticus* will show that any editor of Book II has had to contend not only with manuscript variants but with a rich crop of modern notions about where poems begin and end. The sad result is that of all the poems in a book of 1,362 lines there are only eight, amounting in all to 276 lines, which both have a harmonious manuscript tradition about where they begin and end and which have not been linked with others or themselves split into two or more poems by editors from the fifteenth century on.[1] The problem of what constitutes a poem, and what principles of unity we can invoke is thus sharply posed by Book II in a way in which it is not posed by other books of Propertius.

Some Propertian problems are real, some concocted; this seems a real one. The question of the unity of a poem in Book II is not merely raised by defective division or by disagreement in division among the manuscripts, as similar phenomena do not cause trouble elsewhere. Misled by the invocation of the Muse at 4.6.11, all the manuscripts concur in treating the solemn prologue to the Actium poem as an epilogue to the poem on the bawd; no one doubts they are wrong. The Petrarchan manuscripts link 1.20 and 1.21 because a Gallus is addressed in the first and spoken of in the second, while the Neapolitanus links 1.21 and 1.22 because both refer to the death at Perugia; in all editions these appear as three separate poems. The Petrarchan manuscripts keep hoping that the long elegy 3.11 will come to a stop, and make three poems of it (one indeed has three poems and an epigram); we are sure the Neapolitanus is right in presenting it as a unity. At the end of Book IV, as at the end of Book II, the Neapolitanus' scribe tired of thought and made no break from the beginning of 7 till the end of 11; we hear nothing at this point of 'the generally greater reliability of the Neapolitanus', and with one exception (the manuscripts' separation of 4.8.1–28 from the rest) editors follow the poem division of the Petrarchan tradition. In all these cases we are dealing with poems that no one doubts are distinguishable units, shapely and unassailable. We need to look at more than confusion in the manuscripts to account for the perplexity of editors confronted with Book II.

Problems more like those of Book II do arise in other books, though more rarely. They are problems raised by and often solvable by consideration of the sort of poem Propertius is

[1] The favoured poems are 2, 6, 8, 12, 14, 15, 21, 25.

writing. In 1.15, for instance, at the point where Cynthia must be supposed to intervene and Propertius resumes his tirade with a 'Stop that!' (above, p. 31), it was wrong but not uninstructive of Ribbeck to suggest that we should divide the one poem into two. More difficult still is the question of 1.8, the first 26 lines of which take a theme from Cornelius Gallus and develop it with topics from the *propempticon*. Cynthia is proposing to go to the frozen north as, according to Virgil, Gallus' mistress Lycoris had done; the poet tries to dissuade her and then switches to wishing her well if she is set on going. These lines are addressed directly to her, and so far the development of the poem follows a traditional and conventional pattern, and is tamely servile in its obedience to the precepts of the rhetoricians who gave recipes for such farewell speeches. The next twenty lines, in which Cynthia is spoken of in the third person, are a triumphant reflexion on her determination to stay in Rome; the poet congratulates himself on the help of the Muses and Apollo, that is, on the efficacy of the preceding 26 lines. The two parts of the poem represent two different dramatic moments of the same situation (probably not imagined as widely severed in time); they also present two quite different moods and levels. If nothing else, the position of the poem in the book, framed as it is by two elegies that show a parallel *volte face* in Propertius' poetic friend Ponticus, would suggest that it is a single poem, with a movement from the scholastic to the personal very like that of 1.2 (above, pp. 22 ff.). But its unity has probably been more often denied than asserted, and the reason for the denial, the breakdown of internal dramatic coherence, is one that we shall find operating elsewhere too.

Outside such quasi-dramatic poems problems of a different kind have troubled editors. In Book III, for instance scholars (and scholars of poetic taste like Muretus and Scaliger) have regarded the first two poems as one. This is wrong: both poems deal with elegy and the fame it can give, but they deal with it from quite different points of view and set the central theme off by quite different contrasts (below, pp. 76 ff.); moreover, the first poem begins with an invocation of Callimachus and ends with a pointed allusion to him, so that it has an elegant 'ring' shape. What has caused the trouble here is Propertius' tendency to begin a poem with a word (in this case 'Meanwhile') which suggests that the elegy is a fragment of a conversation or argument of which we overhear only part; and this is a frequent cause of trouble in Book II as well. There is similarly little to be said for the same scholars' attempt to unite the thematically similar but tonally quite distinct 3.4 and 3.5, companion poems, indeed, but not parts of a whole.

Nevertheless, anyone who raised such questions about these particular poems forces us to consider what is the case about Propertius' art with a seriousness that would not be evoked by someone who asked us to envisage the unity of 7–11 of Book IV on the ground that the Neapolitanus presents these poems as a unity. And it is questions of this more crucial kind that are continually posed in Book II; again and again we are forced to ask what criteria of an aesthetic kind we can invoke in trying to decide whether a poem begins here, ends here, is one poem or more.

Only analysis of particular poems can show what is involved, and there is probably no better example for indicating what disputes can arise about the unity of a Propertian poem (not to mention what other considerations have to be borne in mind in attempting to discover what the poet said) than the elegy 2.28. The Petrarchan manuscripts present it as one poem and the Neapolitanus as two (with a break after line 34); perhaps that may by now be regarded as no more than a minor irritation, not indicative of anything.

> *Iuppiter, affectae tandem miserere puellae;*
>   *iam formosa tuum mortua crimen erit.*
> *venit enim tempus, quo torridus aestuat aer*
>   *incipit et sicco fervere terra Cane.*
>
> *Sed non tam ardoris culpa est neque crimina caeli*   5
>   *quam totiens sanctos non habuisse deos.*
> *hoc perdit miseras, hoc perdidit ante puellas:*
>   *quidquid iurarunt, ventus et unda rapit.*

Num sibi collatam doluit Venus? illa peraeque
    prae se formosis invidiosa dea est.   10
an contempta tibi Iunonis templa Pelasgae?
    Palladis aut oculos ausa negare bonos?
semper, formosae, non nostis parcere verbis.
    hoc tibi lingua nocens, hoc tibi forma dedit.

Sed tibi, vexatae per multa pericula vitae,   15
    extremo veniet mollior hora die.
Io versa caput primos mugiverat annos;
    nunc dea, quae Nili flumina vacca bibit.
Ino etiam prima terris aetate vagata est;
    hanc miser implorat navita Leucothoen.   20
[Andromede monstris fuerat devota marinis;
    haec eadem Persei nobilis uxor erat.]
Callisto Arcadios erraverat ursa per agros;
    haec nocturna suo sidere vela regit.
quodsi forte tibi properarint fata quietem,   25
    illa sepulturae fata beata tuae.
narrabis Semelae quo sis formosa periclo,
    credet et illa, suo docta puella malo.
et tibi Maeonias omnis heroidas inter
    primus erit nulla non tribuente locus.   30

Nunc, utcumque potes, fato gere saucia morem;
    et deus et durus vertitur ipse dies.
hoc tibi vel poterit coniunx ignoscere Iuno;
    frangitur et Iuno si qua puella perit.

Deficiunt magico torti sub carmine rhombi,   35
    et tacet exstincto laurus adusta foco;
et iam luna negat totiens descendere caelo,
    nigraque funestum concinit omen avis.

Vna ratis fati nostros portabit amores,
    caerula ad infernos velificata lacus.   40
si non unius, quaeso, miserere duorum.
    vivam si vivet, si cadet illa cadam.
pro quibus optatis sacro me carmine damno:
    scribam ego 'Per magnum est salva puella Iovem';

ante tuosque pedes illa ipsa operata sedebit, 45
  narrabitque sedens longa pericla sua.

Haec tua, Persephone, maneat clementia, nec tu,
  Persephonae coniunx, saevior esse velis.
sunt apud infernos tot milia formosarum;
  pulchra sit in superis, si licet, una locis. 50
vobiscum est Iope, vobiscum candida Tyro,
  vobiscum Europe nec proba Pasiphae,
et quot Troia tulit vetus et quot Achaia formas
  et Thebae et Priami diruta regna senis;
et quaecumque erat in numero Romana puella 55
  occidit. has omnis ignis avarus habet.
[nec forma aeternum aut cuiquam est fortuna perennis;
  longius aut propius mors sua quemque manet.]

Tu quoniam es, mea lux, magno dimissa periclo,
  munera Dianae debita redde choros, 60
redde etiam excubias divae nunc, ante iuvencae;
  votivas noctes, ei mihi, solve decem.

1–4. Jove, my girl is sick; now at last take pity on her. By now if in her beauty she dies the blame will be yours, as the time has come when the scorching air swelters and the earth starts to boil because of the parched Dog-star.

5–8. In fact it is not so much the heat's fault nor the sky's wrong-doing as her own innumerable past impieties. This is what ruins poor wretched girls, now as in the past: all their oaths are the prey of wind and wave.

9–14. Surely Venus did not resent the comparison with herself? She is impartially hostile to all her rivals in beauty. Or did you rather insult Pelasgian Juno's temple? Or venture to say Pallas' eyes are ugly? Always, you beautiful creatures, you don't know how to temper your words; this present sickness of yours is the penalty of your guilty tongue, and of your beauty.

15–30. But for you, storm-tossed through life's many perils, a gentler hour will come at the day's end. Io's head was transformed and long ago she mooed through her early years; now she is a goddess, the cow that drinks Nile's streams. Ino again in her first youth roamed the world; she gets the wretched sailor's prayers as Leucothoe. [Andromeda had been vowed to sea-monsters; she was also Perseus' renowned wife.] Callisto had wandered as a bear through Arcadia's fields; she guides sails by night with her own star. So if the fates do hasten on your rest, those fates of your burial are blessèd. You will tell Semele what being beautiful costs you, and she will believe you, taught by her own disaster. And you among all Homer's heroines will have first place, and undisputed.

31–4. Here and now, wounded as you are, be compliant to destiny; both god and cruel time change. This even his wife Juno will be able to forgive you; Juno too breaks down if a girl dies.

35–8. There is no power in the bull-roarers whirling to the magic spell, and the bay is silent, burnt up on the dead hearth; and now the moon refuses to keep coming down from the sky, and the black bird sings an omen of doom.

39–46. One bark of destiny will carry our loves, sped dark by its sails to the lakes below. If not one, then spare two, I beseech. I shall live if she lives, fall if she falls. In return for this boon I vow to consecrate a song: I shall write, 'My girl is well, saved by great Jove', and she herself will offer sacrifice and sit at your feet, telling the long course of her perils.

47–56. Let this mercy of yours, Persephone, continue, and you, Persephone's husband, be no crueller than she. There are so many thousand beauties with those below; let there be, if possible, one lovely girl in the upper world. You have Iope and fair Tyro, Europa and unchaste Pasiphae, and all the beauties of ancient Troy[1] and Achaea, of Thebes and old Priam's ruined kingdom; and every Roman girl that counted is dead too. All these the greedy fire possesses.

[57–8. Beauty is not a thing eternal nor anyone's fortune perpetual; farther or nearer, each man's own death awaits him.]

59–62. You, my light, since you are let free of great peril, pay the dance you owe Diana, pay too the nights in her temple to the goddess once a cow; those votive nights, alas, pay ten of them.

Almost everything about this poem has been debated, including the question of whether it is one poem or three or four. It is distressing that one cannot operate bluffly with some external criterion, confidently assert, for instance, that there is at least a *prima facie* case for saying that some sixty consecutive lines on one subject are one poem. Like other Augustan poets, Propertius does

---

[1] So the manuscripts; but in view of what follows, any other legendary site would be preferable.

often seek variety in arrangement: the aetiological poems of Book IV are not in a group, but interspersed among others; the two poems to Ponticus in Book I, warning him of the likelihood of love and mocking his fall, are separated by the successful *propempticon* to Cynthia; the first two love poems to occur in Book III frame the elegy lamenting Paetus' death; and there are many other examples of the kind. Unfortunately there are also cases where consecutive elegies, clearly separate, deal with the same subject; in Book II we have 2.14 and 2.15, for instance. Yet unless there is a decided change in the whole treatment of a subject, as there is, for instance, in the three programmatic poems that open Book III, the case for fragmentation perhaps needs more argument than the case for unity.

In the particular case of 2.28, what has led some editors to postulate a plurality of poems is the fact that the situation changes from the beginning, where Propertius' mistress is sick, to the end, where she has recovered. Moreover it is not the same sort of situation change that we saw in 1.8; between Propertius' *propempticon* and his joy at Cynthia's change of mind no more than a few minutes need intervene, but in 2.28 the interval to be assumed between the beginning of the poem and the end is much longer. Two lines can be taken here. Some naively speak as if the sickness must be a real sickness (it might be, of course, but nothing guarantees this), and seem to imagine Propertius reporting on its progress, writing a dozen lines one day and a dozen another, in tones that fluctuate with the course of the disease. With more sophistication, others look for a dramatic unity, seeking and of course not finding some one occasion on which the poet could plausibly address these words to his mistress and the various deities appealed to. In doing this they acknowledge a fact, the links between elegy and comedy; but they are also too respectful of a pseudo-Aristotelianism and of the conventions of most extant Greek drama. An elegy often draws on comedy; that does not mean that any quasi-dramatic elegy can safely be regarded as potentially a fragment of a comedy.

In fact, elegy can deploy many different techniques to represent the social converse of friends and lovers. Some of these techniques

are not dramatic at all, like the epistolary mode of Propertius 1.11
and 2.19.[1] Others, though dramatic, do not fit into the austere
framework of ancient comedy. Of course, an elegy can preserve
the unities of time and place and create a small dramatic vignette
which might be a single speech or one role in a single scene in a
comedy; Ovid does this very often and Propertius fairly often
(for instance, in 1.15, above, pp. 29 ff.). But it can also take a
topic and exhaust it, suggesting at various points particular settings
and times, but refusing to be tied down; a notable example is
Tibullus 1.2, where editors' attempts to find a single dramatic
setting or a coherent series of settings lead to absurdity. Or it can
be discursive, suggesting the speaking voice, but quite unin-
terested in specifying any locale or situation; this is the case with
most of the Propertian poems that begin 'You ask why . . .' Or
again it can, as it seems to do in our poem, comment on and
present a changing situation. In this it may not be so unlike some
ancient drama as accidents of transmission lead us to suppose.

The most living dramatic form in Propertius' day was the mime
or short dramatic sketch. It had been elevated to a severe literary
form by the Hellenistic poet Herodas (who found a Roman
translator early in the first century B.C.), and it profoundly
influenced the *Idylls* of Theocritus and through them the *Eclogues*
of Virgil. In its less strict manifestations it admitted change of
scene (so even in Theocritus 15), or rather, the mime actor could
represent himself in different situations, as 'change of scene'
perhaps suggests change of scenery. In relation to elegy, a mime
of the late first century A.D. is even more interesting than these
more literary Hellenistic examples; it is easily accessible, being
translated and discussed in D. L. Page's *Greek Literary Papyri*,
vol. 1 (Loeb), 1942, pp. 350 ff. This mime presents a developing

---

[1] Before accepting the classification of this poem as a non-schetliastic *propempticon* (Cairns 236 ff.), it is useful to compare its opening words with those of
Cic. *Att.* 5.21, 'I am terribly glad that you have reached Epirus safely and, as you
say in your letter, had the sort of crossing you wanted; but I take it a bit amiss
that you're not at Rome at a time when it is so necessary for me you should be.
My one consolation is that I hope you're having an agreeable winter there and a
welcome rest.' Here, as in innumerable other instances, Cicero's letters give us a
window on to the real social world in which this very social poetry had its genesis.

plot, with some quite startling swings, in eight continuous sections of a total length not much greater than our poem's; in the first seven sections there is only a single speaker, whose words make it plain what the story is and who expresses a variety of emotional responses to its events. The little work shows that the mime at any rate was not bound by the rigid laws of comedy. People used to dramatic performances of this kind would not be over-perplexed if an elegiac poet presented them with different phases of a single situation or even, as Propertius does in 1.8, with an abrupt reversal of a situation. It is overhasty therefore to deny the unity of our poem because it is not set at a particular moment in time, and it would be equally wrong to impugn it because the tone of the poem changes, if it does change. In fact, its tone may vary less than editors sometimes suggest.

Propertius starts with a prayer, to which he returns with greater emphasis and a new argument later in the poem (41 ff.). His mistress has been sick for some while and now that the Dog-days have come it is high time Jupiter intervened; otherwise as god of the weather he will be held responsible for her death. This entertaining sequence is in many editions ruined by the intrusion of lines 33–4 between 2 and 3; the joke is far too good to spoil and it establishes the bantering tone of the whole opening section. The poet exculpates the god (it is not really the weather's fault), and suggests various other causes, his mistress's perjuries, Venus' jealousy of her beauty (at 2.2.13 f. Propertius himself had un-wisely declared his mistress more beautiful than the three god-desses, Venus, Juno and Pallas, who came to the judgement of Paris), an affront to Juno's temple (such an insult had brought trouble on some mythical heroines), an insult to Pallas' looks. For the moment he acquiesces in this: Cynthia's boasting and her beauty are the trouble, and she is the victim of persecution by jealous goddesses.

The poem then takes a new turn, which develops sinuously and in the end invites us to envisage yet another cause and re-establishes Jupiter as the principal culprit. It starts on a consolatory note, promising a fortunate outcome to all this suffering: like others before her his mistress will herself become a deity, of the minor kind called heroine. Why? We are not told directly, but are presented with a set of cases of mortal women persecuted by Juno and subsequently deified. Their stories suggest a better reason for Juno's hostility than an affront to her temple: Jupiter himself is in love with the poet's mistress, as he was once in love with Io, Callisto and Semele.[1] Io comes first, and will be important later in the poem; in her deified form she is Isis, the goddess of Cynthia's devotion (61 ff.), and so a specially suitable example to head the list.

The theme of Jupiter's love for Cynthia is not found only here; in 2.3.30 Propertius said bluntly, 'You will be the first Roman girl to go to bed with Jove.' In our poem the idea is developed with a more characteristic allusiveness, continuing the investigation of the cause of her sickness, providing a consolatory topic and finally suggesting a course of action. Perhaps Jupiter himself is punishing non-compliance with his will ('destiny' the poet grandly calls it, and deflates the highflown concept with a colloquial expression for compliance). Only submission will save Cynthia, a constrained submission that even Juno might forgive. These lines have been much assailed, and the second couplet transferred elsewhere on the assumption that 33 must mean 'this even *your* wife Juno will forgive you'. Editors assert but do not argue for the necessity of this assumption, and the lines seem to arise naturally

---

[1] Semele, though not formally in the list of *exempla*, of course belongs to it; the asymmetry by which she is given a different function from the rest and made the recipient of Cynthia's confidences is a characteristic piece of Augustan elegance. The flat and prosaic couplet on Andromeda has no place in this series, and a few critics rightly eject it (it has the wrong tense in the second line, and unlike the other heroines Andromeda is not deified); it presumably comes from the margin, and may be prompted by the mention of her mother Iope in 51. Ino presents a more difficult problem; some mythographers mention her persecution by Juno, none that she was beloved by Jupiter. In such cases Propertian criticism must hover distracted among four possibilities: (a) this couplet may also be an interpolation; (b) Propertius may have been seduced into an example only partly relevant to his theme; (c) the learned poet may have known of a tradition, inaccessible to us, of Jupiter's love for her; (d) with the same tradition before him as we have, he may have operated creatively on it and assumed or implied the usual motive for Juno's persecution. Editors commonly seem to think (b); in the heir of Callimachus, (c) and (d) are at least as likely (cf. the case of Alphesiboea, above, p. 30 n.1). Choice depends on and eventually determines one's view of Propertius' poetic practice.

from the examples of the previous section, even apart from the fact that they disrupt other contexts into which they are intruded.

The transition to the next section is rather difficult, and is not made any easier by the fact that the manuscripts here contain four lines that are very hard to make sense of in the context of the poem, and that have much distorted its interpretation. The poet or someone else has been practising magic, and the magic has failed. It is assumed that the purpose of the magic is simply to restore Cynthia to health, and so we hear of the poet's 'passionate despair' and of a change of tone 'from fancy to earnest'. One might retort that the picture (no doubt Propertian) of the moon's going on strike and refusing to keep coming down all the time (*totiens*) does not in any case sound particularly despairing or particularly earnest, and that if the poet's magic has failed to save his mistress's life, he seems to be taking the situation rather lightly. This is in itself not at all impossible, and it may point to a right interpretation of the passage; but we have to make a detour to arrive at that interpretation. There is a more serious difficulty about the lines, pointed out by H. J. Rose ('*Ut Pictura Poesis*', *Studia in honorem P. J. Enk*, Leiden, 1955, pp. 167 ff.). These four lines have a rich cluster of associations, in comedy, bucolic, epigram, elegy, and the novel; in all this abundant tradition we do not find this kind of magic invoked for the cure of disease. Its purpose, when one is explicit, is always aphrodisiac or antaphrodisiac, and it is not immediately easy to see the relevance of that at this point. Is the poet trying to win back his mistress's love, cure himself of love for her, or, a more daring exploit, cure Jupiter of love for her? In the contest, only the last possibility seems a starter, and if this is what the poet intended he was asking a lot of his readers, perhaps too much. In such a poem those readers might well expect to find a reference to magic, but to magic of a different kind, the curative singing of charms and lustration with sulphur that Tibullus asserts he employed in Delia's sickness (1.5.11 ff.). If Propertius wrote these four lines for this context, he is substituting for such homely fumigation an antaphrodisiac magic that might hopefully be supposed the remedy for what he has assigned as the real cause of Cynthia's illness. Only some such riddling allusiveness can justify the lines, and if this interpretation is right, the complex wit of the allusion takes us a long way from 'passionate despair'.

In Tibullus' poem his attentive magic is presented as a proof of unequalled devotion, and Propertius' magic similarly eases the transition from the opening section on Jupiter's love to the poet's attestation of his own total fidelity in the prayer to Jupiter in the next lines. The touch is still a light one, consonant with that of the earlier part of the poem. In particular one may note the transformation of an ordinary idea in lines 45 f. It is a commonplace to speak of a prayer and a sacrifice followed by sitting down in a temple. Propertius adds novel details: Cynthia will not just sit in Jupiter's temple; she will sit at his feet and tell him all her troubles. The picture recalls a grand original, the plaint of his beloved Thetis to Zeus in the *Iliad* (1.500 ff.):

She sat down in front of him and seized his knees with her left hand and his chin with her right and begged . . . '. . . Honour my son, who is destined to an earlier death than all others. And now Agamemnon, king of men, has disgraced him; for he has taken away his prize and keeps it for himself.'

In our poem the scene is domestic and enticing, taken to represent a sufficient reward for the god's kindness. It has some parallels in Hellenistic literature, the prayer of the little Artemis on her father's knee in Callimachus' Third Hymn, the posture of Iris by Hera's throne in his Fourth; one may also suspect that there were similar subjects in painting. Yet the boldness and indeed impudence of the allusion to Homer is characteristic of Propertius himself.[1]

At line 47 the poem suddenly veers again, but the connexion is easy enough to see and easy enough to parallel. Propertius turns from what he hopes is now successful persuasion of the god of the sky to the gods of the underworld, independent and dan-

---

[1] So in 1.11.23 f. he expresses his own absorption in Cynthia by adapting Andromache's despairing words to Hector (*Iliad* 6.429 f.), in 4.7 the apparition of the dead Cynthia is modelled on the ghost of Patroclus in *Iliad* 23, in 4.8, where Cynthia bursts in as Propertius is entertaining himself with two dancing girls, wins a notable victory over them and then purifies the house, numerous hints invite us to recall the *Odyssey*. Cf. below, pp. 152–ff.

gerous powers who could cross the will of Jupiter. So far they have spared Cynthia, and he beseeches them not to be greedy to add one more beautiful woman to their kingdom. The prayer is developed with a list of the heroines of the underworld of the kind that haunted Propertius' imagination. The ultimate original is again Homer, in his catalogue of heroines in Book XI of the *Odyssey*, but Propertius adds some *recherché* and modern touches, the Ethiopian Iope to contrast with Tyro's brilliant whiteness, and the anonymous beauties of Rome.[1] The prayer is granted, and Cynthia is urged to pay her vows to Diana and Isis. The description of Isis ('she now is now a goddess, once a cow') already undercuts the solemn pathos with which Propertius had developed the conventional theme of the beautiful dead. The last line expands this mood to an ironical comment on the whole poem. The result of all these successful appeals to various deities is to exclude the poet ten nights more from his mistress's bed. The rueful *diminuendo* restores the mood of the opening lines. This is 'ring-composition' of a particular kind, depending on a turn to the original tone, not to the original subject. In this poem, indeed, Propertius seems to treat the various aspects of his subject matter in a rather high-handed way. Repetition of themes is one of the techniques that elegiac poets use to give organic unity to a poem; here the recurring subjects (the three references to Jupiter, the two to Isis, the two catalogues of heroines) look rather like struts to support the structure, not subtly insinuating a unity, but meant to be seen as elements of the architecture. The organic unity of the poem depends much more on attitude, the continual wry deflation of the commonplaces of love poetry.

Such a poem as 2.28 (if one may by now assume that it is a poem) has a structure much more complex and transitions much subtler and harder to find than anything in Book I or indeed in Books III and IV (with the possible exceptions of 3.7 and 4.3); it

[1] The couplet 57–8 is platitudinous and runs counter to the appeal to Pluto and Persephone to hold their hand. It also distracts one from the procession of the heroines by using the common and therefore masculine gender. Once more, we are left to decide whether the poet has strayed into nonsense or whether someone has scribbled in the margin a reflexion on the inevitability of death vaguely suggested by the context.

seems to exemplify an experiment in technique that Propertius briefly took up and from which he retreated into a manner more naturally congenial to him. In particular, in its use of repetition as a structural element, it recalls the part played by the repetition of thematic words in Tibullus' first book, published in 27/26 B.C. It is of course very unlike a poem of Tibullus, especially in keeping hold of a dramatic structure, however loose. But it seems to aim at a similar unobviousness of connexion, and there is also some similarity of subject matter (above p. 55).

A likeness to Tibullus can also be seen in 2.16, in which Propertius utilises again an idea from the first book. In 1.8 he had shown Cynthia intending to go off to Illyria with a praetor and then thinking better of it. Now the praetor has come back rich, and the poet urges her to accept his gifts and bankrupt him; but from this initial ruthlessness he moves to complaints against her venality and warnings against the god's punishment of infidelity:

> *Praetor ab Illyricis venit modo, Cynthia, terris,*
> *   maxima praeda tibi, maxima cura mihi.*
> *non potuit saxo vitam posuisse Cerauno?*
> *   a, Neptune, tibi qualia dona darem!*
> *nunc sine me plena fiunt convivia mensa,*   5
> *   nunc sine me tota ianua nocte patet.*
> *quare, si sapis, oblatas ne desere messis,*
> *   et stolidum pleno vellere carpe pecus;*
> *deinde, ubi consumpto restabit munere pauper,*
> *   dic alias iterum naviget Illyrias.*   10
> *Cynthia non sequitur fascis nec curat honores;*
> *   semper amatorum ponderat illa sinus.*
>
> *At tu nunc nostro, Venus, o succurre dolori,*
> *   rumpat ut assiduis membra libidinibus.*
> *ergo muneribus quivis mercatur amorem?*   15
> *   Iuppiter, indigna merce puella perit.*
> *semper in Oceanum mittit me quaerere gemmas,*
> *   et iubet ex ipsa tollere dona Tyro.*
> *atque utinam Romae nemo esset dives, et ipse*
> *   straminea posset dux habitare casa.*   20
> *numquam venales essent ad munus amicae,*

atque una fieret cana puella domo;
numquam septenas noctes seiuncta cubares,
   candida tam foedo bracchia fusa viro—
non quia peccarim (testor te), sed quia vulgo   25
   formosis levitas semper amica fuit.

Barbarus exclusis agitat vestigia lumbis—
   et subito felix nunc mea regna tenet.
aspice quid donis Eriphyla invenit amaris,
   arserit et quantis nupta Creusa malis.   30
nullane sedabit nostros iniuria fletus?
   ah, dolor hic vitiis nescit abesse suis.
tot iam abiere dies, cum me nec cura theatri
   nec tetigit Campi, nec mea mensa iuvat.
at pudeat certe—pudeat, nisi forte, quod aiunt,   35
   turpis amor surdis auribus esse solet.
cerne ducem, modo qui fremitu complevit inani
   Actia damnatis aequora militibus;
hunc infamis amor versis dare terga carinis
   iussit et extremo quaerere in orbe fugam.   40
Caesaris haec virtus et gloria Caesaris haec est:
   illa qua vicit condidit arma manu.

Sed quascumque tibi vestis, quoscumque smaragdos,
   quasve dedit flavo lumine chrysolithos,
haec videam rapidas in vanum ferre procellas;   45
   quae tibi terra, velim, quae tibi fiat aqua.
non semper placidus periuros ridet amantis
   Iuppiter et surda neglegit aure preces.
vidistis toto sonitus percurrere caelo,
   fulminaque aetheria desiluisse domo;   50
non haec Pleiades faciunt neque aquosus Orion,
   nec sic de nihilo fulminis ira cadit.
periuras tunc ille solet punire puellas,
   deceptus quoniam flevit et ipse deus.
quare ne tibi sit tanti Sidonia vestis,   55
   ut timeas quotiens nubilus Auster erit.

1–12. The praetor has just come back from Illyria, Cynthia, a great prey for you, a great anxiety for me. Couldn't he have laid down his life on the Thunderbolt crag? Ah, Neptune, what rich gifts I should be giving you then! As it is, the table is full and the banquets go on without me, without me the door stands open all night long. So, if you're sensible, don't abandon the harvest offered you, and pluck the stupid full-fleeced sheep; then when his present's used up and he finishes poor, tell him to sail off again to other Illyrias. Cynthia doesn't trail after emblems of magistracy or bother about office; always what *she* weighs is her lovers' purses.

13–26. But you now, Venus, oh help my pain and make him collapse from uninterrupted love-making. Does just anyone then buy love with presents? Jove, my girl is lost, and for a purchase of no price. She is always sending me to the Ocean to hunt for pearls and bidding me rob gifts from Tyre itself. And indeed I could wish no one at Rome were rich, and that even our Leader could bring himself to live in a hut of straw. Our mistresses then would not be for sale at sight of a present, and a girl would grow grey in one home. You would not be lying seven nights at a time apart from me, your white arms embracing such a beast of a man—not because I did wrong, I call you to witness, but because generally lovely girls always love to be changeable.

27–42. The barbarian stamps, his loins locked out[1]—and now suddenly blessed possesses my kingdom. Think what Eriphyle gained by gifts that brought no joy, how vast the pain in which the bride Creusa blazed. Will no insult calm the storm of my tears? Ah, this pain cannot but attend on the faults that provoke it. So many days have passed since I have felt no love for the theatre, the park, my own table. But I should feel shame at least—yes, to be sure, unless, as the saying goes, a shameful love is usually deaf. Imagine the leader who lately filled with empty din the sea's surface at Actium and doomed his soldiery; he too was constrained by disgraceful love to turn his ships in flight and look for escape at the ends of the earth. Caesar's valour and Caesar's glory is this: he stored away his arms with a hand that was victorious.[2]

43–56. Whatever dresses he has given you, whatever emeralds, whatever chrysoliths with their tawny light, all these I hope to see swept to nothingness by ravaging storm gusts; and may you find them earth, I could wish, find them water. It is not always that Jove is serene

---

[1] I acquiesce in this interpretation of a desperate passage, but with no conviction.

[2] Unless this couplet is totally *à propos des bottes* (by the fault of the poet or, more likely, his manuscripts), something like this must be its sense. Propertius would then be inverting the conventional praise of Octavian's clemency ('Though victorious, he laid his arms aside and did not pursue vengeance').

and laughs at perjured lovers, deaf and heedless of prayers. You have all seen the thunder rushing across the sky and thunderbolts dashing from their home in the fiery air; it is not the Pleiades who do this, nor rainy Orion, and not for no reason, as men think, that the wrathful thunderbolt falls. It is perjured girls that he is usually punishing, since the god himself was taken in and wept. So don't rate a purple dress so highly that you have to feel nervous whenever the South wind brings clouds.

Like much else in elegy, the situation in this poem derives from comedy; it recalls Thais' exclusion of her lover Phaedria in the interests of the braggart soldier Thraso at the opening of Terence's *Eunuchus*. But in spite of this genesis the development of the poem is not a strictly dramatic one. It also matters that Tibullus 1.9, one of the poems addressed to the boy Marathus, has a similar subject matter, the corruption of the beloved by an inferior rival's gifts and warnings against perjury. Propertius seems to be challenging comparison with this poem, and he has once more chosen to operate in a Tibullian way. Here too this mode of writing has led to the poem's unity being questioned, and scholars have broken it up into two or three poems, as well as shuffling the lines about to produce a more acceptable coherence. But the poem has a good deal in common with 2.28: once more, a shifting situation is envisaged, there is no single occasion on which the poem could be uttered, direct address to Cynthia alternates with mention of her. This poem also depends on thematic recurrences, and these have here a common feature: on its first appearance each is represented as what should be the case, on its last as what is the case. We have the storm at sea in which the praetor should have perished, the storm that should sweep away his gifts, the storm with which Jove does punish perjury. The cliff on which the praetor's ship should have been wrecked is the cliff of the Thunderbolt (*Cerauno*, not the standard form of the name); at the end of the poem the thunderbolt does not fall without reason, but is hurled by the angry Jove. Rome's Leader should live in a hut of straw, a model of frugality; instead a Leader, if not the Leader, created a great fuss about nothing and was a signal example of the power of disgraceful love. All three of these topics seem to be

fused in the reference to the 'empty din' with which Antony filled
the sea at Actium. Jove is appealed to at 16 and displays his wrath
at 47 ff. The lover's ears are deaf to his own disgrace (36), the
god's are not always deaf to prayer (48). These repetitions span
the poem and give its motley emotions a formal coherence.

An elaborate instance may confirm that in this elegy Propertius
has Tibullus in mind. It was a commonplace of ancient poetry that
the gods do not attend to lovers' vows and that they can safely
forswear themselves; Tibullus used the conventional thought at
1.4.21 ff., in another of the Marathus poems:

> *Nec iurare time: Veneris periuria venti*
> *irrita per terras et freta summa ferunt.*
> *gratia magna Iovi; vetuit pater ipse valere,*
> *iurasset cupide quidquid ineptus amor.*

And do not be afraid to swear: Love's perjuries are swept by the winds
over land and the sea's surface and brought to nothing. Great thanks to
Jove; the father himself decreed invalid all that foolish love should
swear.

In 1.9.11 f. he also prayed for the destruction of the gifts that
captivated Marathus:

> *Muneribus meus est captus puer. at deus illa*
> *in cinerem et liquidas munera vertat aquas.*

My lad was ensnared by gifts. May the god turn them to ash and clear
water.

Propertius seems to pick up both passages, the winds from one,
the conversion to ash and water from the other, and use them as a
transition to a characteristic inversion of the commonplace about
lovers' vows (2.16.43 ff.):

Whatever dresses he has given you, whatever emeralds, whatever
chrysoliths with their tawny light, all these I hope to see swept to
nothingness by ravaging storm gusts; and may you find them earth, I
could wish, find them water. It is not always that Jove is serene and
laughs at perjured lovers . . .

The complex allusion is, in the ancient manner, the acknowledg-
ment of a debt, and in this poem the debt is due to more than

individual passages. It is also a challenge, and shows how little likely Propertius was to subdue his imagination to the generality and his style to the admirable plainness of Tibullus, even when the formal similarity was greatest. Every idea is transformed: the vivid particularising of the gifts enhances their splendour, their metamorphosis to earth and water is to be the result not of the god's action but of Cynthia's judgement, the conventional paradox of the immunity of lovers' perjuries is taken to be no paradox, but a scientific generalisation admitting exceptions, the exceptions being attested by experience. This is the ground of the warning in the splendidly comic final couplet:

So don't rate a purple dress so highly that you have to feel nervous whenever the South wind brings clouds.

Tibullus is at this point cruelly outdone; but the poem would not be at all as it is if he had not written.

And yet about both these poems, for all their brilliance and inventiveness, one can be forgiven for feeling 'clever ape' or, better perhaps, 'elegant chamaeleon'. The testimony that there is something imperfect is precisely the fact that their unity has to be demonstrated, the function of the structural props pointed out. In 2.16 particularly the formal patterning imperfectly masks an emotional incoherence: the *personae* of the anguished lover and the affectionate but disengaged adviser, objective about his own folly as well, are here shown to us side by side with no more than elaborate symmetries to glue them together. Similar phenomena in Tibullus insinuate a harmony that leaves us in no doubt that it *is* a harmony; even though we may sometimes feel puzzled about how precisely, having started at A, we have got to B, A and B are equally authentic, and authentic on the same level. This manner, in fact, is not altogether natural to Propertius and his total success with it is intermittent. In other books he develops in almost all his poems a strongly articulated architecture, where solid paragraphs are juxtaposed. One paragraph may develop from another or stand in contrast to it, as the initial thought suggests that investigation of its opposite would be handy or entertaining; a paradox may be piled on another, an argument backed by a set of examples. But in Book II paragraph often shifts into paragraph without the relation between them being at all plain or the rhetorical organisation clearly marked. Many of the difficulties that have been found in the book stem from this difference of approach; a reader with a taste for Propertius' other work is likely to find many poems in II inconclusive or fragmented. Yet where it succeeds, and particularly where it has been brought to harmony with Propertius' own favourite role of the passionate but objective self-observer, this more associative progression perhaps better mirrors the processes of feeling than the argumentative development that Propertius uses elsewhere, and Book II contains some of his greatest love poems, some of them generating a brooding intensity that is hard to parallel in ancient poetry.

It is worth giving one in full, without much further comment, because it both displays the perfection of this manner and provides an instructive contrast with 1.1 (above, pp. 14 ff.). Here too Propertius defines his own situation by opposites, the figure of the happy and credulous lover (not a rival, whatever editors say), the band of those who are philanderers on principle. He also contrasts his state with that of the happy lovers of old. The elegy thus has several points of similarity with the earlier one; but the starts into new ideas and, in particular, the density of the imagery create a poem of a quite different kind. The poem is instructive in another way too: because Propertius' love poetry is so good and presents, at its best, situations so strongly imagined, he has been credited with a truth to mere fact that has sent his editors into strange paths of biographical construction; this poem (2.25), in which he so powerfully declares his unique bondage to the unique Cynthia, has a companion piece (2.22A in Barber), the antecedent of Donne's *The Indifferent*, in which he presents himself as a hopelessly susceptible philanderer.

The poem, one of the most perfect in Book II and one of the lucky few whose unity is undisputed, may be allowed to speak for itself:

> *Vnica nata meo pulcherrima cura dolori,*
> *excludit quoniam sors mea 'Saepe veni',*

ista meis fiet notissima forma libellis,
   Calve, tua venia, pace, Catulle, tua.

Miles depositis annosus secubat armis,   5
   grandaevique negant ducere aratra boves,
putris et in vacua requiescit navis harena,
   et vetus in templo bellica parma vacat;
at me ab amore tuo deducet nulla senectus,
   sive ego Tithonus sive ego Nestor ero.   10

Nonne fuit satius duro servire tyranno
   et gemere in tauro, saeve Perille, tuo?
Gorgonis et satius fuit obdurescere vultu,
   Caucasias etiam si pateremur avis.

Sed tamen obsistam. teritur robigine mucro   15
   ferreus et parvo saepe liquore silex.
at nullo dominae teritur sub crimine amor qui
   restat et immerita sustinet aure minas,
ultro contemptus rogat, et peccasse fatetur
   laesus, et invitis ipse redit pedibus.   20

Tu quoque, qui pleno fastus assumis amore,
   credule, nulla diu femina pondus habet.
an quisquam in mediis persolvit vota procellis,
   cum saepe in portu fracta carina natet?
aut prius infecto deposcit praemia cursu,   25
   septima quam metam triverit arte rota?
mendaces ludunt flatus in amore secundi;
   si qua venit sero, magna ruina venit.

Tu tamen interea, quamvis te diligat illa,
   in tacito cohibe gaudia clausa sinu.   30
namque in amore suo semper sua maxima cuique
   nescio quo pacto verba nocere solent.
quamvis te persaepe vocet, semel ire memento;
   invidiam quod habet non solet esse diu.

At si saecla forent antiquis grata puellis,   35
   essem ego quod nunc tu; tempore vincor ego.
non tamen ista meos mutabunt saecula mores;
   unus quisque sua noverit ire via.

At vos qui officia in multos revocatis amores,
  quantus sic cruciat lumina vestra dolor!   40
vidistis pleno teneram candore puellam,
  vidistis fuscam; ducit uterque color.
vidistis quandam Argiva prodire figura,
  vidistis nostras; utraque forma rapit.
illaque plebeio vel sit sandycis amictu;   45
  haec atque illa mali vulneris una via est.
cum satis una tuis insomnia portet ocellis,
  una sat est cuivis femina multa mala.

1–4. You who alone were born most lovely to be the concern of my
pain, since my fate excludes the words 'Come often', that beauty of
yours my books will make best known, with my apologies, Calvus, by
your leave, Catullus.

6–10. The soldier full of years lays aside his arms and lounges in
retirement, aged oxen refuse to pull ploughs, the ship rests rotting on
the empty sand and the old war shield is at ease in a temple; but as for
me no old age will withdraw me from your love, whether I turn out a
Tithonus or a Nestor.

11–14. Would it not have been better to be the slave of a hard
tyrant and sob in your bull, cruel Perillus? Better indeed to have been
turned to stone by the Gorgon's countenance, even to suffer the
Caucasian birds.[1]

15–20. All the same I shall hold out. Rust wears away the sword
edge, steel though it is, and a little water the flint. But no reproach
from a mistress wears away a love that stands firm and endures listening
to undeserved threats, that comes to beg when spurned, confesses its
fault when injured, and returns of itself with dragging feet.

21–8. As for you, who put on haughty airs in the flood tide of love,
credulous fool, no woman is steady for long. Does anyone really pay
his vows in mid storm, when the keel often floats shattered in the
harbour? Or claim the prize when the race is unfinished, before his
wheel has skilfully grazed the turning post for the seventh time?
Favourable winds in love are sportive liars; when a house crashes late,
it crashes in force.

29–34. Meantime, however much she loves you, keep your joy close
clutched to you and say nothing. For in a love that is one's own it is

---

[1] The eagle that tormented Prometheus by eating his liver, the locale, in
ancient physiology, of sexual passion.

always one's most boastful words that somehow or other do the damage. However often she invites you, remember to go only once; nothing that provokes envy ever lasts.

35–8. But if these were the days loved by the heroines of old, I should be what you now are;[1] it is the times that defeat me. Yet the age we live in shall not change my ways; each man must know how to go his own path.

39–48. Those of you who call your services to attend on many loves, how great an anguish then torments your eyes. You have seen a young girl all fair, you have seen a dusky one; both complexions attract you. You have seen a Greek woman walking in public, you have seen our Roman girls; both figures make you rush after them. Never mind whether she dresses in working clothes or scarlet; this path or that is the same entrance path for the cruel wound. Since one woman is enough to bring sleeplessness on one's eyes, one woman is a multiple pain enough for anyone.

---

[1] Credulous and haughty, obviously, though the point is sometimes missed. But this is all we have been told about him, and therefore all that is relevant.

CHAPTER THREE

The Quest for Callimachus

IT is characteristic of the older poets of the Augustan age to boast of a peculiar kind of originality, the conquest for Roman literature of a genre already perfected in Greek. The claim did not originate with them; it is present already in the boast of Ennius (about 200 B.C.) to be the reincarnation of Homer, the first Roman who had climbed the cliffs of the Muses and bothered about perfection of style. It is expressed also by Cicero in his attitude both to Demosthenes and to the Greek philosophers; especially indicative for the meaning of such claims is the defence of philosophy in Latin in the proem to the *De Finibus* (1.6 f.):

So if Greeks read Greeks writing on a different principle on the same subject, why should not Romans read Romans? Indeed, if I just translated Plato and Aristotle as our Roman poets have translated plays, should I be conferring a small benefit on my fellow citizens in importing those godlike geniuses for them to know? That I have not so far done, and I do not suppose it forbidden ground either. I shall import some passages if I so decide, and especially from the authors mentioned, whenever it happens to be appropriate; so Ennius does from Homer, Afranius from Menander.

Few Romans were as capable as Cicero of being explicit about the principles they followed, but this is a fair description of the practice of the Augustan poets too.

Several things in the passage are noteworthy. First and foremost is the proud consciousness that the Romans had now succeeded in the heroic enterprise on which, alone among all the peoples with whom the Greeks came in contact, they had embarked nearly two centuries before: they had made Latin into a classic language, and Cicero was its first classic author, the first Roman writer whom Greeks could not afford to neglect. No other people but the Jews, whose literary tradition ante-dated

Hellenism, could ask the self-confident question, 'If Greeks read Greeks . . . why should not Romans read Romans?' The second is the notion of public service, rendered even by adequate translation of Greek ideas. The third is the rejection of translation as an insufficient ideal and its replacement by the concept of original composition, on which Greek influence was profound but discriminately and consciously admitted; it is relevant here that Cicero takes as his example of a comic writer not Plautus or Terence or any of those who retained a Greek setting for their plays, but Afranius, who transposed them to the Italian scene. All these elements recur in the Augustan claims for their own new poetry.

In Virgil and Horace the claim assumes a stylised form, the boast of innovation being coupled with an allusive reference to the author imitated:

My Muse was the first that deigned to sport in the Syracusan verse (of Theocritus).

I sing through Roman towns the Ascraean song (of Hesiod).

I shall be called the first to bring to Italian strains the Aeolic song (of Alcaeus).

I was the first to display to Latium the Parian iambs (of Archilochus).

It is a notable fact about elegy that we find no such thing either in Tibullus or in the early books of Propertius. Whether because the Greek genre, the epigram, that elegy derived from was so minor or because of the poets' consciousness that Roman elegy as it had developed did not owe its form to any Greek poet, love elegy did not choose to represent itself as the result of a successful plundering expedition, proudly displaying the trophies of conquered tribes.

In his first book Propertius mentions the utility of Mimnermus as the model for the poet in love, but he does not in any sense claim Mimnermus as his own poetic ancestor; and though the situation in 1.18 is borrowed from Callimachus (Gallus of course may well have intervened), and though the story of Hylas in 1.20

had been told by Apollonius, Theocritus and Nicander, no comparison with any of them is invited. In 2.1 he uses the Callimachean apology for not writing epic (below, pp. 73 f., 91 f.), and mentions Callimachus' well-known refusal to thunder as a precedent for his own disabilities; but the topic was by that time in any case conventional in Augustan poetry. At the end of the book a reference to Callimachus and Philetas makes the same point as the mention of Mimnermus in Book I: Lynceus in love would be better advised to imitate them than the philosophers and grand poets, epic and tragic, who have hitherto engaged him. When at the end of the poem Propertius details his own literary lineage, it is a purely Latin one; the Virgil of the *Eclogues* has predominance, and the Latin love poets follow (2.34.85 ff.):

> *Haec quoque perfecto ludebat Iasone Varro,*
> *Varro Leucadiae maxima flamma suae;*
> *haec quoque lascivi cantarunt scripta Catulli,*
> *Lesbia quis ipsa notior est Helena;*
> *haec etiam docti confessa est pagina Calvi,*
> *cum caneret miserae funera Quintiliae.*
> *et modo formosa quam multa Lycoride Gallus*
> *mortuus inferna vulnera lavit aqua!*
> *Cynthia quin vivet versu laudata Properti,*
> *hos inter si me ponere Fama volet.*

This was the sport of Varro when he had finished his Jason, Varro, his Leucadia's violent flame, this the tuneful theme of the writings of Catullus that make Lesbia better known than Helen herself, this the avowal of learned Calvus' page when he sang of poor Quintilia's death. And how multiple the wounds caused by beautiful Lycoris dead Gallus lately washed in the waters of the Underworld. Yes, Cynthia too shall live, praised in Propertius' lines, if Fame shall choose to place me among these.

At this period that is the canon to which Propertius seeks entry, and this in spite of the fact that some aspects of his style in Book II, particularly in its use of a series of flashing and distinct images (cf. 2.25, above, pp. 64 ff.), seem already to show the influence of Callimachus in a more profoundly assimilated form than the poems of Book I. It is only in Book III, however, that he asks for initiation into Callimachus' rites, only in Book IV that he hopes his Umbria will be known as the home of the Roman Callimachus and earns, from Horace of all people, a bad tempered rebuke for his presumption (*Epist.* 2.2.91 ff.):

I compose odes, he elegies. 'A work marvellous to see, engraved by the nine Muses.' See first with what haughty airs, what effortful striving we stare around Apollo's temple bare of Roman bards. Later, if you have the time, follow us and eavesdrop on what each claims, why each entwines a garland for his head. We belabour each other and wear out the enemy blow for blow, regular Samnite gladiators in a long drawn out contest till the lights are brought. His vote makes me an Alcaeus; and what does mine make him? What but a Callimachus? If he seems to claim more, he becomes a Mimnermus, and swells with the title he longs for. I put up with a lot to placate the touchy race of poets . . .

It was not Propertius who had set that particular ball rolling.

When Propertius turned to thinking of himself as a possible Roman Callimachus, he was on the point of ceasing to be a love poet. Only about a third of the poems in Book III are love poems, and two of those are a farewell to love poetry. Much of the book has an investigatory air and the poet seems to be exploring his own capacities and trying to define what he took poetry to be. The first five poems form a group which examines the claims of epic and elegy and their relation to war and peace, but is principally interested in the poetic nature of Propertius himself. There had never been a time when Propertius was not aware of Callimachus as a master of erotic themes and a model in the use of myth and allusiveness, irony and surprise. More recently he had developed a highly imaged style that owes still more to the Greek poet. But in this investigation of his own poetic talent he was inevitably deeper in debt to him, and redefined his aims with Callimachus' help. But this rethinking, though it gave him a more exact understanding of Callimachus and a terminology to express an ideal of poetical style, did not yet lead him to the imitation of Callimachus' poem. The elegies of Book III remain in scale and shape Roman elegies of the by now traditional form. Their content though was profoundly modified, and so was their style.

Once more, what turned him in this new direction seems to

have been an impulse imparted by another poet, on whom the influence of Callimachus' style was, though in another genre, pervasive. One does not with Propertius have the impression of dealing with a poet in whom the urge to creativity was an uncontrollable passion. After the achievement of the *Monobiblos* and probably of the first part of Book II, it looks as though something external was necessary to rouse him from periods of silence. In this particular case the something external was the appearance, in the second half of 23 B.C., of the three books of Horace's *Odes*. The influence of the *Odes* is so diffused throughout Book III that one can conjecture that a good many of the poems were written after 23 B.C., in other words, that Propertius had not written much since 26 B.C. Even apart from the Paetus elegy, which has affinities with an eccentric Horatian poem (below, pp. 86 f.), the coincidences are many. A central and recurrent topic of Book III is the praise of the life that shrinks from money-making; it is not quite new in Propertius (cf. 1.6), but it is nowhere else dominant, and it is characteristically Horatian. Some treatments of it, 3.5 in particular, have frequent linguistic similarities with the *Odes*. The same is true of the equally central topic of poetry's ability to confer immortality, where again the end of 3.2 owes images to *Odes* 3.30. The hymn to Bacchus (3.17) is an elegiac rehandling of themes in Horace's two Bacchic poems, 3.4 is in form, if not in tone, related to *Odes* 3.14 and also exploits some suggestions of *Odes* 1.29 (below, pp. 105 ff.), while the use of a not very relevant myth, related at length, to point a contemporary moral in 3.15 reminds us of Horace's Hypermestra and Europa odes (3.11, 3.27) and is very different from the elegant tightness of application that Propertius had given to the myth of Hylas in 1.20. It is in style, however, that the effect of the *Odes* is most striking, and most of all in the brilliant and often violent use of successive metaphors that Horace learnt from Callimachus. Surprisingly, it seems that the eye of the Roman Callimachus was turned to a sharper contemplation of his great exemplar by the influence of the Roman Alcaeus; that might account for Horace's bad temper.

Two passages of Callimachus are important to the opening poems of Book III. One we have long known, the ending of the hymn to Apollo (105 ff.), where the poet defended himself against detraction:

Envy whispered in Apollo's ear, 'I hate the bard whose song is not as multitudinous as the sea.' Apollo kicked Envy and said, 'The stream of Assyria's river is wide, but for the most part it sweeps down offscourings of earth and abundant rubbish. It is not from everywhere that her priestesses carry water to Demeter, but from that which creeps along pure and undefiled from a sacred spring, a tiny trickle, the top of perfection.'

The other passage, possibly more significant for Latin poetry than any other single page of Greek, is the preface to the *Aetia*, in which the aging Callimachus brilliantly states his poetical creed. Apart from scattered fragments, it was unknown fifty years ago and the text is still here and there defective. It is worth attempting a translation of a reconstructed text that is occasionally provisional, since in spite of its importance it is not even yet thrust enough on the attention of readers of Latin poetry; and mere mention of it is no substitute for the extended acquaintance that alone shows why its impact on the Augustans was so tremendous:

Wizard craftsmen often squeak at my poetry, ignoramuses who are not the Muses' friends; they complain that I have not finished off one continuous poem many thousand miles long in honour of kings or heroes of olden times, but unroll my verse only a little distance, like a child, though the decades of my years are not few.

I say this to them: 'Prickly race, who know nothing but how to wear your own hearts out with envy, all right, my lines are few; but Philetas' *Demeter* far outweighs his long old woman,[1] and of the two it is his little poems that show Mimnermus agreeable, not his great girl. Long be the flight from Egypt to Thrace of the crane that delights in the Pygmies' blood, and long be the shot the Massagetae direct against a Mede; nightingales are sweeter as they are. Off with you, destructive race of the Evil Eye; learn to judge poetic skill by art, not by its leagues of length. And do not look for me to breed a loud-sounding minstrelsy; thundering is Zeus' trade, not mine.'

---

[1] If this text is right, the reference would be to the hypothetical *Bittis* (above, p. 10), while Mimnermus' 'great girl' is his elegiac sequence, the *Nanno*. But the supplement is here very doubtful and the allusions unclear.

For when first I set my writing tablet on my knees, Apollo said to me, he of Lycia:

'Dearest of poets, feed your sacrificial offering as fat as may be, but keep your Muse, dear fellow, slim. And this too I bid you, to tread where wagons do not trample, not drive your chariot on tracks that others share nor on the broad highway, but on unworn paths, even though the way you drive be rather narrow.'

I obeyed him: as a poet I am one of those who love the cicada's shrill cry, and have not come to like the din of asses. Let another bray like the long-eared beast, and may I be the slight creature, the winged one, ah just that, so that old age, that dew—that that food down dropping from the bright air I may eat and sing,[1] and strip off that other,[2] that lies heavy upon me like the three-cornered island on deadly Enceladus . . . For those whom the Muses have not looked askance at in youth, they do not rebuff in old age. When the swan can no longer stir its wing, it is then its song does its work best.

At this point the text, which has been becoming more and more fragmentary, ceases to present more than scattered words. We know however that Callimachus went on to talk of Helicon, the Boeotian mountain on which Hesiod was, he tells us in the preface to the *Theogony*, consecrated as a poet by the Muses themselves, that he represented himself as dreaming that he too was on Helicon, that he spoke of the spring Aganippe and of the river Permessus at the foot of Helicon, which was connected with Aganippe; he may also have mentioned the fountain of Hippocrene higher up just below the summit of the mountain. He certainly told how in his dream he met the Muses, who gave him the subject matter of the *Aetia*.

From these passages Roman poets, starting from Ennius, derived a series of images of great poetic power to express the poet's dedication to his art, the dream on Helicon or Parnassus, from which the poet brings down a garland (not a myrtle wand as in Hesiod) that is the symbol of his poetic consecration, the sacred grove, the untrodden paths, the undefiled spring, the song of the swan. We also find in them the contrast between the spring of Hippocrene, grand and remote, the fountain of the epic poet,

[1] The ancients believed that cicadas fed on dew.
[2] Old age.

and the humbler Aganippe or Permessus in the valley, appropriated to lower genres of poetry. Already in the Sixth Eclogue, his own most complete intimation of the nature of poetic power, Virgil had shown Gallus, presumably as the author of the *Amores*, wandering down by the banks of Permessus and led up on to Helicon by one of the Muses to the choir of Apollo and her sisters; there the divine shepherd Linus gave him the pipe of Hesiod and commanded him to write an epyllion on the Grynean grove. In apologising for his present inability to sing of Augustus in 2.10, Propertius had taken over this image and applied it to himself (25 f.):

> *Nondum etiam Ascraeos norunt mea carmina fontis,*
> *sed modo Permessi flumine lavit Amor.*

My songs do not yet know even the Ascraean spring, but Love has bathed them only in the stream of Permessus.

He recurs to it again in 3.1 and 3.3, but the images are now much more complex and less conventional.

The first poem opens with the invocation of the shades and rites of Callimachus and Philetas: the poet begs for access to their grove and in terminology familiar but more hyperbolical than usual claims to be the first to come from the undefiled spring as a priest of poetry to carry Italian mystic emblems in Greek dances. The mystic emblems (*orgia*) belong to enthusiastic cults like that of Dionysus; the poet is the officiating priest who will reveal the new religion to his compatriots and initiate them into it. The image of the poet as priest goes back beyond Callimachus to his grand original Pindar, who declares himself, in the language of the Delphinian cult of Apollo, the spokesman of the Muses, the shaping craftsman who interprets and makes intelligible the wild promptings of inspiration. We are some way from that attitude here, with in the background a religious world both more fervid and less rational. The varied images generate and express an excitement that is heightened by a series of eager questions to Callimachus and Philetas; though the poet has much to reveal, he also has much to learn. What was the mountain glen in which they spun their poems so fine? which the lucky foot they entered with? what the spring they drank from? We are given no direct answer to these questions, and need not look for one. The poet is asking for help, not here mapping out a programme.

Instead he strikes out on another track; if he has not learnt everything Callimachus and Philetas could teach him he has learnt some things. At any rate, the work of the poet of war is excluded for him. Verse polished with refining pumice is his aim, and is what already gives him glory. A swift succession of shifting images expresses the glory, each fading into the next like a set of cinematic exposures. Fame soaring high above the earth raises the poet (is she a bird, a winged goddess, or a winged chariot?); then the chariot of his Muse is that of a Roman *triumphator* with the little Loves, his poetic children, riding beside him, and the crowd of writers following, the subordinate officers and common soldiery of his poetic army. In the next instant the chariot has become a racing chariot that other poets are vainly trying to pass, and in the last image a chariot on the narrow open road, not to be overtaken. Callimachus' aversion from the wagon track and the common path is taken further than he thought of: it is not just that the high road should be avoided; there is no high road to the Muses, and the poets who think there is are doomed to fail.

Not that they are few: 'Many, Rome, will add your praises to record'[1] and sing of the future conquest of the East. The book this poem introduces is something different, one to be read in a mood of peace, one brought down from Helicon by an untrodden path. Ennius had claimed the same, and that he brought down the poet's garland to prove it; that will not suit Propertius:

> *Mollia, Pegasides, date vestro serta poetae;*
> *non faciet capiti dura corona meo.*

Soft, Muses of Hippocrene, be the wreath you give your own poet; a hard garland will not suit my head.

The self-conscious delight in delicacy is the guarantee of poetic dedication.

---

[1] *annalibus*, with a reference to the Roman tradition of historical epic, which had its model in Ennius' *Annales*.

It cannot, of course, guarantee a poet from detraction in his lifetime, but it will secure him glory after death, which is the only time people get it anyway. People keep on saying that it is Homer's song that preserves the renown of the Trojan war, but that is nonsense. What makes the Trojan war glorious is its antiquity. For that matter, what makes Homer himself glorious is his antiquity. And time will do as much for Propertius. Of course, time alone would not do it, but the poet has done his part, and Callimachus' god, the Lycian Apollo, has assented to his vows; he can afford to wait.

Might time, one might ask, not do as much for the wars of the present as it had done for the war of Troy and cast over them too the glamour of heroic antiquity? Virgil thought so, and with a jump of imagination beyond any other Roman poet foresaw a time when the peasant of the future, cultivating the fields of Philippi and Pharsalia, would marvel at the huge bones of the heroic dead, outsize memorials of an age of legend like the bones of Orestes and Theseus disinterred by their pious successors in the sixth and fifth centuries B.C. (*Georg.* 1.493 ff.). Such Epicurean pessimism about the continuing enfeeblement of the human race demanded a profounder disenchantment than Propertius could deploy. Moreover, he thought he knew the motive of contemporary warfare, greed for cash, and he found it vulgar. He had not been told that the Trojan war was 'really' a struggle for trade routes in the area of the Dardanelles; like Homer, or like himself, the Trojan war, he thought, deserved its posthumous renown. A great poet could fitly sing about that, but not about the wars of the present.

Poetry is in fact too powerful and too precious to be misapplied; so the second poem proceeds. It has a magical power of conciliation: Orpheus could enchant beasts and rivers, Amphion make rocks move to form the walls of Thebes. The conventional examples are followed by one presented as even more remarkable: poetry attracted the beautiful Galatea to the one-eyed giant Polyphemus. No wonder Propertius is the centre of a bevy of admiring girls; he has something to offer, even though he falls below the level of acquisitiveness the age demands. Callimachus

had complained in the third of his *Iambi* that his age valued
wealth above merit; in particular, his own poverty lost him the
love of the boy Euthydemus, whose mother found a richer lover
for him. Propertius was more fortunate. He lacks, he says, the
delights of a fine Roman house and villa (described, as so often,
in an affectionate detail that reveals a taste for what it condemns:
no columns of *verde antico*, no coffered ceiling of gold and ivory,
no orchards rivalling those of Alcinous, no elaborate water works
extravagantly fed with the best drinking water, *Marcius . . .
liquor*); but he has the company of the Muses. The pattern of
argument is an old one, starting in Bacchylides, deployed by
Lucretius and Virgil to celebrate the pure joys of the life of the
countryside, and most recently by Horace to assert that his poetic
power won him the friendship of the great and his Sabine villa,
enough to content him (*Carm.* 2.18.1 ff.). The patronage of the
Muses has given Propertius something else, the power to confer
undying fame on his mistress. Once more the fame is merited
(3.2.16):

> *Carmina erunt formae tot monumenta tuae.*

My poems will be so many memorials of your beauty.

The beauty, we must suppose, does exist; it too is a proper
subject of song.

The third poem takes up the themes of the previous two, the
rejection of historical epic and the restriction to love poetry.
Directly challenging comparison with Callimachus, it uses the
motif of the dream that the poet is on Helicon. Ennius had
already exploited it, and in his dream the shade of Homer had
appeared to him, told him the doctrine of transmigration of souls,
and acknowledged Ennius as his own reincarnation. So naive a
confession of indebtedness is not in the Augustan manner;
Propertius does not encounter the shade of Callimachus that he
had invoked in 3.1.1, nor is he escorted by Ennius. Instead we
have an allusion to Ennius' achievement and an account of
Propertius' meeting with Apollo and the Muses. In the prologue
to the *Aetia*, Apollo's warning was not part of the dream, as it is
in Propertius. Indeed, the section containing it (above, p. 74)

may be a new prologue to a second edition of the *Aetia*, which in
the original version perhaps had only the dream of the meeting
with the Muses. Yet Propertius is not the first to think of the
warning as given in a dream; Horace had already made the combination in the *Satires* (1.10.32 f.), where Quirinus appeared in a
dream and warned him that for an Italian to write Greek verses
was insanity. Certainly the connecting of the two visions, linked
by a vivid description of the grotto of the Muses, enhances the
dreamlike atmosphere in Propertius' poem. Scene replaces scene
rapidly and completely, and an air of inconsequence is convincingly created.

At the opening of the dream Propertius is eager to sing the
exploits of the kings of Alba Longa[1] and he has been trying to
bring his lips near to the great fountain (of course Hippocrene)
from which Ennius had drawn the inspiration for his epic on
Roman history; some episodes of the *Annales* are recalled, not in
order and one of them indeed not belonging to it.[2] The poet is
checked by Apollo, who warns him against ambitions too high for
him; the great ocean of epic is too turbulent for Propertius' skiff.
Instead the god points with his ivory plectrum to the end of a new
path over mossy ground; it is a grotto, and detail after detail of it
is presented as the poet surveys it. Each of the details is sharply
concrete, the green grotto with its mosaic, Bacchus' *tympana*
hanging from the hollow pumice, the Muses' mystic emblems, the
clay mask of Silenus, Pan's pipes, all symbols of ecstatic poetry.
Probably it all seems more strange and wonderful to us than to a

---

[1] In the Callimachean passage at the beginning of the Sixth Eclogue, Virgil had
represented himself as trying to sing of 'kings and battles' till rebuked by Apollo;
the Alban kings, his ancient commentators tell us, perhaps with their eye on our
passage. This is surprising, in view of their general neglect of the elegists.
Certainly, no one ever seriously projected an epic on the kings of Alba Longa, a
dim line of shadows invented to fill a chronological gap.

[2] Line 8 'the royal trophies brought to Rome on Aemilius' ship'; surely no
Roman would take this to refer to anything but the most famous of the triumphs
of the Aemilii Paulli, that over Perses of Macedon in 167 B.C. It happened two
years after Ennius' death, and so the editors present us with other less conspicuous Aemilii. It is perhaps simpler to believe that Propertius did not quite get
to the end of Ennius' 18 books. Paullus' triumph *would* have been a suitable climax
to the *Annales* if fate had so decreed.

Roman, who saw many such things in the gardens of civilised villas and town houses; like the pose of Apollo when Propertius first becomes aware of him, 'leaning by a grotto on his gilded lyre', and like the picture of the doves drinking that follows, the images belong to art (below, p. 165). They are no less dreamlike for that.

The picture of the grotto culminates in the water it contains, the water that Propertius is to drink and that will consecrate him as a love poet. Its epithet *Gorgoneus* shows it to be still the water of Hippocrene (Propertius does not think there is first and second class inspiration, the *grand cru* of Hippocrene and the bourgeois growth of another spring), but here it is contained in an artificial basin, not gushing out in a great stream, and even Venus' doves can dip their beaks in the water that Propertius could not get his mouth to at the fountainhead. The inspiration is no less authentic, but it is tamed and civilised.

The spring is succeeded by a vision of the Muses, whose tasks are different like the different kinds of poetry over which they preside. One singles herself out; her beauty shows her to be Calliope, mother of Orpheus. She reiterates the warning of Apollo: no contemporary epic; Propertius is to be content with a chariot drawn by swans, the birds of Venus (and of Callimachus). But, more kindly than Apollo, she gives the poet positive advice: he is to sing of lovers' serenades at their mistress's door. He need not despair of being useful to society either; those who want to do down the stern puritans of Rome will learn from him how to charm even close-kept girls out of doors. She fetches the water and moistens his lips to dedicate him to his new task.

How much of the detail of the poem is Callimachean we cannot tell; it is not even perfectly certain, though it is hard to doubt, that the consecration by water was already in the *Aetia*. But Calliope's advice must be Propertius' innovation; it is only in the context of Roman society that the attribution of utility to love poetry has point and wit. The challenge to Roman *mores* is deftly delivered but real, as Ovid recognised. For him the image of consecration had lost its power, and in the preface to the *Ars* he mocked it mercilessly; but the claim of high didactic purpose is renewed (1.25 ff.):

I shall not lie that you taught me skills, Apollo; no bird on the wing gave me advice; I never saw Clio and Clio's sisters as I herded my sheep in your valleys, Ascra. Utility prompts my work. Believe the bard; he is expert.

Better for him if he had been able to veil the boast of being useful to immoralists in the safer guise of Calliope's advice.

The fourth and fifth poems of the cycle move the argument further into the area of life and society that it approaches at the end of the third. Like 3.1 and 3.2 they are a contrasting pair, so that we have a double frame round the third poem, which is thus marked off as Propertius' central statement. The first deals with war, the other with peace, and the opposition is deliberately marked: *arma* 'war' is the first word of 3.4, *pacis* of 3.5; in the first line of each, a patron deity is assigned them:

> *Arma deus Caesar dites meditatur ad Indos.*
> *Pacis Amor deus est; pacem veneramur amantes.*

War is what the god Caesar is planning against the rich Indians.
Peace has Love as its god; peace is what we lovers worship.

But war and peace are here considered not as themes for poetry, but as ways of life. Both poems see the motive for war as the desire for gain. The poet rejects acquisitiveness and militancy, in favour of love and poetry now while he is young and, less convincingly, in favour of natural philosophy, which he reserves for his old age (3.5.19 ff.):

> *Me iuvat in prima coluisse Helicona iuventa*
> *Musarumque choris implicuisse manus;*
> *me iuvat et multo mentem vincire Lyaeo,*
> *et caput in verna semper habere rosa.*
> *atque ubi iam Venerem gravis interceperit aetas,*
> *sparserit et nigras alba senecta comas,*
> *tum mihi naturae libeat perdiscere mores . . .*

It is my delight in youth to have haunted Helicon and linked hands with the dancing Muses, my delight too to fetter my mind with abundance of the god of release[1] and always have spring roses round

[1] The wine god.

my head. And when burdensome years cut Venus off and white old age
besprinkles my black hair, then let me choose to learn the ways of
nature . . .

We are indeed hardly even meant to be convinced by the aspira-
tion towards philosophy, expressed as it is in terms wickedly
reminiscent of Virgil's abdication from philosophy and resort to
poetry as a *pis aller* in the second book of the *Georgics* (475 ff.):

> *Me vero primum dulces ante omnia Musae,*
> *quarum sacra fero ingenti percussus amore,*
> *accipiant caelique vias et sidera monstrent . . .*
> *sin, has ne possim naturae accedere partis,*
> *frigidus obstiterit circum praecordia sanguis,*
> *rura mihi et rigui placeant in vallibus amnes;*
> *flumina amem silvasque inglorius.*

But for me first of all may the sweet Muses whose sacred emblems I
bear, astounded with enormous love for them, welcome me and teach
me the paths of heaven and the stars . . . But if I am checked from
approaching these regions of nature by the chill of the blood round my
heart, let me choose the countryside and running streams in the valleys
and without fame love the rivers and woods.

Propertius develops the passage at tedious length (Roman poets
had an inexplicable fondness for lists of potential research subjects
in natural philosophy), but its point seems to lie in these first few
lines. Virgil alleged as the cause of his incapacity for philosophy
the stupidity resulting from the chill of the blood round his heart;
a different chill, that of old age, is what will turn Propertius to it.
It is philosophy, not poetry, that is for him the *pis aller*. Virgil was
older, possibly more than twenty years older; perhaps he had
forgotten the delights of triumphant youth and what it was to
dance with the Muses on Helicon.

   This programmatic cycle is firmly marked off as such by the
first of the few love poems of the book that recall the manner of
the earlier ones; it has a companion piece of the same breed in 3.8.
The pair of them frame a bizarre and troubling poem, the elegy on
Paetus, which is a new departure in Propertius, resuming contact
with the poetic world of Greek epigram that had provided the

starting point of many of the earlier poems, but treating it in a very different way. In Book II hardly any poems are an extension of epigram of the kind we find in Book I (above, pp. 13 ff.); the unimportant 2.30 is perhaps the only certain example, since 2.23, though it has a parallel in the *Anthology*, deals rather with a theme common to diatribe and satire (most recently in Horace, *Serm.* 1.2), the superiority of the love of accessible whores to more complicated liaisons. Moreover, even in searching for coincidences of detail between Book II and the *Anthology* all that the industrious Enk can collect is unimpressive, and very few poems are relevant, the enquiry into Cupid's nature (2.12) and the ecstatic celebrations of a night spent in love making (2.14, 2.15). In 3.7 the situation is very different, and different also from what we find in Book I; the lament invents a structured story and a character for Paetus,[1] and encrusts it with a mosaic of commonplaces from epigram.

Paetus is a merchant drowned at sea, a death of peculiar horror to the ancient world, partly because of the devouring of the body by fish, partly because it was in any case likely to entail that the dead man would not be buried. The seventh book of the *Palatine Anthology* contains a great number of poems on the subject, of which a late epigram by Julianus comes nearest to summarising the drift of Propertius' poem (*Anth. P.* 7.586):

It was not the sea and the winds that destroyed you, but insatiate love of insane commerce. May I have a modest livelihood on land; let others pursue gain from the sea, won by fighting the gales.

This is the motif that Propertius states with great energy in the first part of the poem, deploying as well other themes common in the *Anthology* poems: the dead man is food for fish, the gulls are near where he lies, the sea itself is his grave. Yet there is more emphasis on the motive of greed than we find anywhere in epigram, and the poem is thus linked in attitude and subject to 3.5:

---

[1] That it invents some detail is obvious, that it invents more likely. Editors sometimes suppose that Propertius had an eyewitness report of how Paetus' ship broke loose from the rock; it is not easy to see why.

Ergo sollicitae tu causa, Pecunia, vitae,
  per te immaturum mortis adimus iter,
tu vitiis hominum crudelia pabula praebes;
  semina curarum de capite orta tuo.
tu Paetum ad Pharios tendentem lintea portus   5
  obruis insano terque quaterque mari.
nam dum te sequitur, primo miser excidit aevo,
  et nova longinquis piscibus esca natat.
et mater non iusta piae dare debita terrae
  nec pote cognatos inter humare rogos.   10
sed tua nunc volucres astant super ossa marinae,
  nunc tibi pro tumulo Carpathium omne mare est.

So it is you who are the reason for life's anxiety, Money, you who make us enter the road leading to early death, you who give bloody nurture to men's vices; the seeds of ambition spring from your stock. You, when Paetus spread his sails for Alexandria, overwhelmed him again and again in a furious sea. In following you, the poor wretch lost his life in his first youth and now floats, a strange food for far-off fish. His mother cannot pay the due rites of loving burial nor inter him where the bodies of his kin were burned. And now the seabirds stand above your bones, and the whole Carpathian sea counts as your tomb.[1]

These opening 12 lines could themselves be an epigram, though one of more complication and intensity than most. But the poem develops from the point it has now attained. The address to Paetus begun in the last sentence is continued explicitly[2] and in

---

[1] The Carpathian sea is between Rhodes and Crete. In Augustan poetry such geographical references are not to be taken literally, and we should not suppose ourselves able to infer that Paetus was sailing to Alexandria by a route that took him between Rhodes and Crete; Alexandria is mentioned as a typical rich market, the Carpathian as a typical dangerous sea, and that is all.

[2] Between the first address to Paetus ('And now the seabirds . . .') and the vocative use of his name the manuscripts have an excited reproach addressed to the North Wind and another addressed to Neptune. Neither coheres very well with the immediately following statement that the sea has no gods, and the address to Neptune contains an unwanted eulogy of Paetus' crew ('The men that hull carried were holy'), while the use of *timor* in the rarish sense 'cause of fear' both in line 13 and in line 28 could be a reason why a reader scribbled the lines 13–16 in the margin. Yet in this exclamatory poem the abrupt changes of addressee are perhaps justifiable, and both the North Wind and Neptune recur in the later section of the elegy that takes up themes from this part. No similar defence is available for 21–4, which can only be defended by mis-translating them.

terms that anticipate the later development of the poem. He is told there is no point in saying how young he is, and speaking of his mother; the sea has no gods to hear him, and the ropes that tied his ship to a rock have been chafed by a night storm and broken. Other epigrammatic themes, the prayer that he may be cast ashore and find burial and the comment of the ship's captain who passes the tomb, close this second section. Once more the poem is at a possible stopping point:

> *Et quotiens Paeti transibit nauta sepulcrum,*
> *dicat 'Et audaci tu timor esse potes'.*

And whenever a ship's captain passes Paetus' tomb, let him say, 'You can cause fear even in the bold.'

The next part of the poem is a tesselation of gnomic utterances on the dangers of the sea, many of them commonplaces of the *Palatine Anthology*. They are developed with a variety of expression, ironical command, indignant question, downright and economical statement, that is rhetorically very effective, even though its rhetoric is that of the declamatory schools, not of real oratory. Equally rhetorical is the use of two examples to close the section, the destruction of the general Greek fleet on its return from Troy and the series of disasters that overtook Ulysses' crew. Another motif of epigram and of rhetoric, the contrast between farmer and sailor, enlarges the example of Ulysses. If he had been content to plough his ancestral lands, he could have lived at home feasting in comfort (as Penelope's suitors did), not rich but with nothing but the absence of riches to bewail.

This return to the opening theme of the poem, the greed for wealth, brings us back to Paetus. He was much less adapted to the seafarer's life than Ulysses; four lines express his delicate youthfulness and the luxury in which he travelled, four more the horrors of his wreck, his nails torn out by the roots as he was swept off the raft drifting in the night. Then a lyrical speech put into his mouth recurs to the themes of the second section: he appeals to the gods of the sea, points out his youth, wails that he will be dashed on the lonely rocks where halcyons nest and that Neptune has used his trident against him, begs that he may be cast up on Italian shores, so that his mother can bury him. Those were his last words.

A coda follows, *diminuendo*. The goddesses, since not the gods, of the sea, the Nereids and Thetis, should have pitied him and propped up his weary[1] chin; he would have been no weight. The tender regret is cut across by a couplet designed to clash with it by way of finale:

> *At tu, saeve Aquilo, numquam mea vela videbis;*
> *ante fores dominae condar oportet iners.*

But you, cruel North Wind, shall never see my sails; it is before my mistress's door that I must lie unseen, no man of action.

It is this couplet alone that attaches the poem to love elegy.

As often with Tibullus, musical metaphors are natural when talking of the lament for Paetus, and in its use of repetition the poem recalls, though with more finished artistry, the techniques of some of those in Book II. Yet both in its subject and in the particular way it uses epigrammatic motifs it is not of Tibullus that the poem most reminds us, but of another exercise in the bizarre and baroque, the Archytas ode of Horace (1.28). There we find an address to the long-dead philosopher king Archytas by what, we at length become aware, is an unburied victim of shipwreck, who finally urges a passing ship's captain to bury him; and we also find that over much of its length the poem depends for evocative effect on a mosaic of epigrammatic themes. The Paetus elegy and the Archytas ode are among the most imaginative of Augustan poems outside Virgil, and they operate with many similar commonplaces and use them in a similar patterning way. The same technique, that is, is being applied and in each case is being applied to a strongly imagined situation, though to very different effect. However profound his influence on Propertius' style in this book, Horace did not in general have much to say to his imagination. The Archytas ode, however, is eccentric among Horace's poems. Its structure is more open than most, partly

---

[1] Propertius uses the elegists' *lassus*, edged with sentiment, not the grander *fessus*.

because it is written in lyric couplets, not stanzas (it is worth noting that in 3.22 Propertius again acknowledges a debt to the equally epodic ode 1.7); in some of the *Odes*, notably 2.12, Horace in taking up Propertian topics seems intent on emphasising by contrast what he took to be the tedious discursiveness of elegy, but in the epodic poems he himself took more room. Moreover, the ode's vivid, not to say gruesome, suggestiveness was not alien from the elegiac manner. However misleading the talk about Propertius' 'obsession with death', it is nevertheless true that in dealing with it his imagination drew on unusually rich stores of imagery and suggestion (cf. above, pp. 35 f.). It looks as though he responded to something akin in the Archytas ode, and learned more than one lesson from it. Far more than the rather mechanical epicedion on Marcellus (3.18) or the much admired poem on the dead Cornelia (4.11, see below, pp. 145 ff.), the Paetus elegy presents us with an harmonious and unobvious structure, informed by an eloquent lyricism that we shall not often find Propertius so unselfconsciously master of.

Two love poems (3.8 and 3.10) again frame a complex poem to Maecenas (below, pp. 109 ff.); like 3.6 (and 3.16) they are gay and elegant pieces, carrying on the line of the earlier books, given a dramatic context and development and moving within its framework. Only a misapprehension of Propertius' earlier manner can see in any of these poems a special foreshadowing of the more complex comic triumph of 4.8; their considerable virtues of dramatic vigour and ironical objectivity were virtues that Propertius had had from the beginning.

On the other hand, he does try to open new ground in 3.11, the first of a series of apparently experimental elegies (11, 13, 14, 19), none of which is really successful, in spite of some beauties of detail. They are nominally still love elegies, and most of them present themselves, like many of the earlier poems, as the poet's speech in a particular situation; a conversation has been going on, of which we now hear part. But in these poems this supposed situation is of no interest to him or to us, often reducing itself to little more than a preliminary formula of the 'You ask ...' or 'Why be surprised ...?' kind. It is important to be able to distinguish

here between formulaic and imaginative uses of formulae.
Propertius begins 2.1 with the words:

> *Quaeritis unde mihi totiens scribantur amores,*
> *   unde meus veniat mollis in ora liber;*
> *non haec Calliope, non haec mihi cantat Apollo.*
> *   ingenium nobis ipsa puella facit.*

You are all asking what is the cause for my writing of love so often,
what the cause why my book is so insinuating in its progress to fame;
it is not Calliope, not Apollo who dictate my themes. My genius is
produced just by my girl.

With this he evokes, in this first poem of Book II, the success of
Book I and his own excited reaction to it. Historical truth is not
necessarily involved (that is, the sentence does not *prove*, though
it suggests, the prior publication of Book I), but an imaginable
and realistic situation is being presented. That the poet then loses
interest in his imagined public and becomes absorbed in his present
theme is equally intelligible; it is, after all, represented as being
completely absorbing. But no such possible background explains
the idle curiosity of the interlocutors of 3.13:

> *Quaeritis unde avidis nox sit pretiosa puellis,*
> *   et Venere exhaustae damna querantur opes.*
> *certa quidem tantis causa et manifesta rapinis:*
> *   luxuriae nimium libera facta via est.*

You are all asking why girls are so avaricious and a night costs so
much, and why wealth, drained by Venus, complains of loss. There is a
sure and obvious explanation for all their piracy: the path to luxury is
now too unencumbered.

If it is so obvious, why ask? And anyway, why ask Propertius
particularly? And who are these people who cannot see obvious
explanations? The irrelevance of such questions to the context
reveals that the formula has here become a perfunctory verbal tic
which will, it is hoped, give dramatic life to a poem otherwise
short of it.

   These four poems are in fact rhetorical developments of general
topics ('Why can women subjugate their lovers?', 'Why do girls

nowadays cost so much?', 'Is male or female lust greater?'), and they remain on the level of generality, with none of the dramatic power of the love poems in his earlier manner. Moreover the development of the topics is often derivative and unconvinced, like the Cleopatra episode of 3.11, which owes something to *Odes* 1.37, or the praise of the primitive life in 3.13, which is not only decked with rather inorganic reminiscences of Lucretius, Virgil and Tibullus, but inserts, as an instance of the way gods and goddesses used to speak to human beings, a translation of a pretty epigram by Leonidas. The most entertaining of these poems is 3.14, a paradoxical commendation of the Spartan *régime*, not, as was normal, for encouraging the military virtues and stern sobriety, but for making girls exercise naked in the gymnasium, a blessed contrast with the chaperones and overdressing of Rome; yet even this is better in idea than execution. Mostly, they show an exhaustion of the genre, and give the impression that the poet is bored with love poetry and trying, though as yet unsuccessfully, to find new modes. The series extends as far as 3.19 and is broken by poems of other kinds, the reproach to Postumus (below, p. 108), which begins promisingly but sinks into a mistaken attempt to tell the story of the *Odyssey* in a dozen lines, two 'Horatian' poems (3.15 and 3.17), a love poem in the earlier style (3.16), and a lament for the death of young Marcellus, Augustus' nephew and son-in-law (3.18). In all this part of the book perhaps only the slight but amiable 3.16 and the hymn to Bacchus (3.17) avoid the tedium inescapable in the spectacle of a good poet in an impasse and looking for both a subject and a manner.

The last set of poems, 20 to 25, may again be a cycle, though with some puzzling features. The first, which in style is certainly of this period and not earlier, first urges and then exults at the beginning of a love affair. The mistress's name is not mentioned, but explicit reminiscences of earlier commendations of Cynthia make it hard to believe that she is not intended. The poem is a difficulty for those who believe that Propertius simply recorded the events of his love affair as they happened and also for those who, though they take a less naive view of the relation of his poetry to experience, think that his aim was the novelettish presentation of the stages of his love and disillusion. In fact it seems to be here to contrast with poem 21, in which Propertius, not more than a quarter seriously,[1] expresses his intention of abandoning Cynthia and setting off to Athens, and also with the two poems that at the end of the book make up an *envoi* to love and love poetry. It is worth noting that the poet apparently had to write for Book III a poem with the dramatic date of Book I (above, pp. 41f.).

Propertius' professed intention of setting out for Greece is not only contrasted with the poem that precedes it, but has a pendant in 3.22 in which he urges Tullus, the dedicatee of Book I, to return from Asia Minor, where he presumably remained after going out on his uncle's staff in 30 or 29 B.C. For Propertius Rome is the scene of an unhappy and disgraceful love affair and his cure will be found abroad, a solution rejected as useless in 1.1 (above, p. 16); for Tullus it is remaining abroad that will be a disgrace. Propertius develops the poetical theme of the praise of Italy (we are meant to remember the *Georgics* and *Odes* 1.7) to persuade him home; she is Tullus' motherland and the fairest place on earth. But that is not the only reason why he should return; in Italy he can pursue the official career his birth demands, find an audience for political and forensic eloquence, marry and continue his line, do in fact all the things that in Italy are impossible for Propertius. The two poems together are intended to make us think of 1.6, in which Propertius refuses to accompany Tullus to Asia and sets up a series of contrasts between himself as the hopeless slave of love and that promising and active young man.

Poem 23 is an amiable *jeu d'esprit* in which Propertius laments the loss of his writing tablets in terms that imply they are dead, and in view of the gender of *tabellae*, presumably dead slave girls who had served him faithfully and could win women over almost

---

[1] Critics speak of his 'misery'. It is not easy to see this in a poem in which he first professes that at Athens he will study the most difficult of all philosophies in the Academy, then retreats to the easier doctrines of Epicurus, then to the study of rhetoric, then to the reading of comedy, and ends with 'Or anyway I shall look at the pictures and statues'. This is far too agreeable and orderly a progression to mirror the distraction of a mind in torment. The lines that make the poem into a love elegy are by contrast fairly chill.

by themselves. In the opening section the allegory is plain to a Roman ear, and this jest may be a prime reason for the poem's existence:

> *Ergo tam doctae nobis periere tabellae,*
> *scripta quibus pariter tot periere bona. . . .*
> *qualescumque mihi semper mansere fideles . . .*

And so my clever tablets are lost and so many virtues, written ones, with them . . . Such as they were, they were always loyal to me . . .

Horace shows what the colloquial pattern was in the *Satires* (2.5.101 f.):

> *Ergo nunc Dama sodalis*
> *nusquam est. unde mihi tam fortem tamque fidelem?*

And so my dear friend Dama is no more. Where shall I find another so brave, so loyal?

Apart from their own good qualities a message from his mistress has been lost with them (one sent a letter on wax tablets and got back a reply on the same set); perhaps it was a message of reproach, perhaps an invitation, perhaps just gossip. And now the charming creatures may be used for a business man's accounts and kept among dreadful[1] daybooks. Moved at the thought, the poet offers a reward and sends a slave boy to post up a notice of their loss.

There seems no particular reason why this cheerful trifle should stand where it does. Williams suggests that we are meant to see a reminiscence of Catullus 42, where the poet summons his hendecasyllables to demand his notebooks back from a woman who is detaining them. He apparently attaches importance to a reminiscence of Catullus at this point, near 20, a late-placed poem on an early stage of the love affair (like Catullus 51). But if Propertius meant the reader to think of Catullus 42 he has given him remarkably few clues to the allusion. Judging by his imitation in *Amores* 1.12 Ovid at any rate missed it; the ordinary Roman reader must have stood an even slimmer chance. A desire for

---

[1] 'Ludicrous overemphasis' said Housman in commending the alternative reading 'harsh'. No; comic hyperbole.

variety of tone before the two rejection poems seems as much
reason as one can find for the elegy's position.

Like 3.21 and 3.22, the first of the rejection poems recalls the
first book and with another deliberate reminiscence of 1.1
declares itself the close of a career in poetry that opened there:

> *Quod mihi non patrii poterant avertere amici,*
> *eluere aut vasto Thessala saga mari,*
> *hoc ego non ferro, non igne coactus . . .*

What my father's friends could not avert from me, nor a Thessalian
witch wash away with all the vast sea, this I (have got rid of), not
constrained by surgery or cautery . . .

Yet he perhaps gives a clue, as the poem goes on, that this farewell
to love poetry is not a farewell to poetry *simpliciter*. More than
most of the poems in the book, this one deploys the new Horatio-
Callimachean style. Almost insolently the poet exploits his new-
found manner in a series of startlingly diverse images, as dazzling
and inconsequent as those of 3.1. He has been shipwrecked on the
sea of love, roasting in Venus' bronze (perhaps a riddling allusion
to Perillus' bull, cf. 2.25, above, p. 66), a captive with his hands
bound behind his back. But now his ship is garlanded and come
to harbour, he has crossed the dangerous and distant shoals and
cast anchor. He is resting from travel and his wounds have healed
over. He dedicates himself to his saving goddess, Good Sense, as
Jupiter has refused to hear his prayers. This set of new fireworks
is the more conspicuous for being followed by a more conventional poem, and one more indebted to epigram, invoking on
Cynthia the curse of old age; the new and the old in his poetic
manners are self-consciously juxtaposed and set each other off.

The book deserves a lengthy and complete analysis, because it
is one of the rare ancient books in which we can see a poet
consciously (and rightly[1]) discontent with what has so far
brought him success and repute, striving for a new manner but

---

[1] Rightly, as we can see from the subsequent development of what had hitherto
been the dominant form of Roman elegy. If a poet of the sparkling and inventive
genius of Ovid could do no more with it than he did in the *Amores*, the possibilities
of the genre were indeed exhausted.

only intermittently successful in finding one. The book opens with the 'portico gleaming from afar' that Pindar had urged on poets, and it contains other good poems. But for all its ambition and successes, its author was in a predicament unlike that of other Augustan poets. Neither Horace nor Virgil stopped still in poetry, but in their unremitting attempt to recreate forms that would again make accessible to poetic handling areas of emotion and action that it had long given up, what they did was move from genre to genre, and all of these genres were already established except for Horace's last invention of the *Epistles*. People knew what to expect of a bucolic, didactic or epic poet, a satirist or a lyrist; the Augustans gave them more than they expected but could at any rate build on a framework of assumptions. Elegy was of its nature more fluid and inchoate. Gallus and Propertius after him had created one way of saying in it something Roman and relevant and had imposed a form on it. But that had not exhausted its possibilities; both in subject and in scale there was more to be discovered. On the other hand elegy did, in all its diverse manifestations, impose a tone of voice; for a poet intent on remaining an elegist there was less stylistic freedom than for one who could move into a new genre to say a new thing. What the limits of the elegiac manner were, what range it could be extended to cover, was not obvious. Propertius had, without yet attempting to break the Roman elegiac form, tried some extensions of subject matter in Book III. But that was not enough, it appears, to satisfy ambitions that he had begun to conceive.

Propertius' predicament moreover was not merely a formal one; it involved as well a question of the range of subject matter not merely possible, but desirable, and this part of his predicament was profoundly entangled with his attitude to the Augustan *régime*. That is why, in the first poems of Book III, he links the antithesis between a refined and Callimachean style and the epic, an antithesis inherited from Catullus and the other poets of the last age of the Republic, with the second antithesis between peace and war. Virgil and Horace might have come to believe that the Augustan *régime* was some guarantee of peace, though even here we should be careful of an easy assent; the end of the first book of the *Georgics*, read to the *princeps* in 29 B.C., shows how tenuous Virgil's hopes long were and how tardily his comfort came if it did come, while Horace reconciles his longing for civil peace with patriotic suasions to chastise foreign enemies. Propertius' enthusiasms were less divided; he saw little merit in turning on the Parthians the weapons that Rome's citizens had ceased to turn on each other, and in echoing Horace's commendations of the simple life he also took pains to point out that the desire for military conquest sprang precisely from discontent with the simple life. However much he might wish for a wider subject matter than he had hitherto deployed he still wanted to write poetry to be read in a mood of peace, and that excluded subjects that the older poets could regard as their domain.

It is in this area that one of the most subtle and thoughtful of recent analysts of the Augustan view of the poet's role seems to have got Propertius profoundly wrong. Newman in his discussion (op. cit., p. 172) complains that though Propertius has assumed the stance of the grand and inspired poet, the *vates*, a concept excogitated by Virgil and of great importance to both him and Horace, he has not understood what it implies:

He has accepted the theory that poets have a new dignity more reminiscent of the great days of Greece than of Alexandria, but he has failed to grasp that this dignity carries with it any particular social responsibility, and he is using the *vates*-concept along with references to Callimachus and Philitas as if it were merely part of the Alexandrian apparatus . . . But all Propertius really had of the *vates* was the feeling of his own importance. Nowhere is the power of Alexandria more evident. It just prevents Propertius from thinking in any other categories except those of the personal and intimate style on the one hand and the grand manner on the other. That one could combine Callimachus and a revival of the grand manner seems scarcely to have entered his head.

There is an element of truth in this; that is, it does seem likely that in Book III Propertius did not clearly disentangle the problem of form and the problem of subject matter, and in his central statement in 3.9 (below, pp. 109 ff.) there is perhaps still some muddle. But Newman's critique seems erroneous in two ways. First, since it is precisely in this book where he is exploring the possibility of a grander manner and a wider subject matter that Propertius liberally acknowledges a debt to Callimachus and prays for his aid, it does not seem probable that Newman has diagnosed the trouble in saying 'That one could combine Callimachus and a revival of the grand manner seems scarcely to have entered his head'. Secondly, and more to the point, Propertius has no such easy answer as Horace to what constitutes 'social responsibility', though he certainly grasped that this concept of the poet carried a demand for social responsibility. It was because he grasped this that he tried at the end of 3.3 a witty parry of the demand (above, p. 80); but though that works in terms of a single poem and though some at any rate might think precepts of seduction as socially responsible as commendation of Parthian wars, it was of course not an answer to be content with. On the other hand responsibility to the society of a civilised Rome and a civilised Italy demanded more than a return to the simple virtues of 'the manly stock of rustic soldiery, trained to turn over clods with Sabine mattocks' that Horace praised (*Carm.* 3.6.37 ff.); Horace's own poetic practice acknowledged as much, however much it sometimes conflicted with what he said. What subject matter that left for the peaceful poet was a question that it took Propertius time to solve, if indeed he can be said to have solved it. But even if 'solve' is inapplicable, at any rate from his vantage point in a younger generation he came nearer to diagnosing the despairing dilemma in which his successors found themselves. Love, friendship, philosophy, antiquarianism, the pursuit of formal perfection and a subtle artistry for its own sake, these are the solutions we have found and shall find him suggesting. Could an imperial poet safely go outside them, unless he wanted to join the herd of minor eulogists? When the greatest poet of the next century aimed at a more public theme, he was forced to commit suicide for treason at the age of twenty-six.

There is no point in attributing prescience to Propertius, but some point in considering what his attitude to the *régime* was, why he was conscious of being himself in a dilemma about it, and why he was probably never clear that social responsibility involved promoting its ideals, as Newman seems to imply. To see why this is so it is necessary to look first at the sort of person Propertius was.

Unlike the older Virgil and Horace, the elegiac poets all belonged to that class of the Italian aristocracy which had not sought advancement in a political career at Rome, but had been long content with local dominion. We are told of Ovid and Tibullus and can, given his other connexions, be sure of Propertius, that they were *equites Romani*, and the Propertii seem, like the Ovidii, to belong to the local baronage of Italy. In Book IV the astrologer Horus tells Propertius that his family was well known and defines the limits of his *patria* (4.1.121 ff.):

> *Vmbria te notis antiqua penatibus edit.*
> *mentior? an patriae tangitur ora tuae,*
> *qua nebulosa cavo rorat Mevania campo*
> *et lacus aestivis intepet Vmber aquis*
> *scandentisque Asisi consurgit vertice murus,*
> *murus ab ingenio notior ille tuo?*

Ancient Umbria is your mother and your household well known. Do I lie? Or does one touch the edge of your native land where misty Mevania is dewy with its hollow plain and the Umbrian lake grows warm in summer and Assisi's wall rises on the hill as it climbs, that wall your genius makes more renowned?

Mevania is the modern Bevagna with its small cupped plain in the hills west of Foligno (the reference in *cavo . . . campo* is probably so locally precise, not to be extended to the whole plain of Assisi). The Umbrian lake is probably the marsh in which the Fiume Chiascio used to lose itself, north-west of Assisi, though others, reading *non tepet* for *intepet*, see a reference to the springs of the Clitumnus well to the south, halfway between Bevagna and Spoleto; on the second hypothesis Propertius' *patria* would have a quite startling extension, on the first the three points delimit the rich plain of Assisi with some of its surrounding hills, an area larger than the territory of a single city. This is quite big enough in all conscience, and in its location it is consonant with what Propertius says in 1.22:

> *Si Perusina tibi patriae sunt nota sepulcra,* . . .
> *proxima supposito contingens Vmbria campo*
> *me genuit terris fertilis uberibus.*

If you know the graveyard of our country at Perugia, . . . Umbria bore me where it touches it at its nearest point in the plain below, a land rich in fertile fields.

A *patria* so extensive was hardly the patrimony of one branch of the *gens*, even though estates were bigger in Umbria and Etruria than elsewhere; how large Propertius' family estate proper was we cannot know, but he tells us it was considerable (4.1.129). As one would expect of large land owners in this area, at least one connexion of the family took the wrong side in the civil war between Octavian and L. Antonius that broke out because of the Italian protests against the seizure of land in 41 B.C. to resettle the veterans of Philippi and that culminated in the destruction of the neighbouring Perugia. Some of the land of Propertius' own family was confiscated (4.1.130), and south of Assisi Octavian settled the military colony of Hispellum (Spello), with a large territory that included the springs of the Clitumnus, even if it did not continuously stretch so far.

Yet at least one branch of the family continued very prosperous, rich enough to support one of its members in the official career. This was C. Propertius Postumus, the recipient of 3.12, who rose to a praetorship and proconsulship and married the daughter of Aelius Gallus, the adoptive father of Tiberius' minister Sejanus. We come here on a significant nexus of family relations. Sejanus' natural father, Seius Strabo, belonged to a family of a similar rank to the Propertii, from Vulsinii in South Etruria; Seius Strabo's mother was a member of the noble Roman family of the Terentii and the sister of Maecenas' wife. Maecenas himself of course belonged to the same class of local magnates, a principal family of the North Etrurian Arretium (Arezzo).

To people of this standing a political career at Rome, praetorian anyway and consular with luck, had long been open if they chose to pursue it, as Propertius Postumus did, as Ovid, against the pressure of the Emperor, refused to do, as Maecenas, following the tradition of his family, ostentatiously disdained to do. This social status is important in estimating the attitude of the elegists to the Augustan *régime*, and in the interpretation of particular poems. We tend too much to take our picture of patronage from the relationship best known to us, that between Maecenas and the freedman's son Horace, and to limit what Propertius or Ovid might have said by what Horace might have said. In a society so status-conscious as that of Rome Propertius and Horace can never have regarded themselves, nor have been regarded by Maecenas, as standing in the same relation to him. Though the elder Cato had expressed one ideal of the Roman state when he said, 'Rights, law, freedom, political action are the common property of all, repute and office the reward of individual effort', the different ideal stated by Scipio Aemilianus was, at any rate in its upper levels, more consonant with fact: 'Innocence is the source of worth, worth of office, office of command, command of freedom.' Talents and address could do much, and for Horace they did a great deal; but they could not do so much as status to support the desire to speak freely. Increasing autocracy of course made a difference; a hundred years later almost anyone could more safely be outspoken than a high-ranking senator.[1] But in this first generation of the empire the Roman and municipal aristocracy had not yet been thoroughly terrorised.

Propertius' first book was published, we have seen, later than the crowning mercy of Actium in September 31 B.C. (above, pp. 42 f.). Yet in the relevant years of the early twenties, when Virgil at the end of the *First Georgic* and Horace in, for example, *Odes* 1.2 were hailing Octavian as Rome's divine saviour, Propertius' book contains one mention only of his name and not a friendly one. As the last poem but one he put an epigram recalling

---

[1] Juvenal in the first satire could get away with the courageous cynicism of 'Well, if satire of the living is not safe I'll try what I'll be allowed to say against the dead', but at the same date the consulars Tacitus and Pliny were having to produce nauseous encomia on the blessed age of Trajan as one where one could once more freely say what one thought. Few availed themselves of the proffered liberty.

the murder of a Gallus after his escape 'through Caesar's swords' from besieged Perugia in 41 B.C. And in the last poem of all, telling of his own origin, he makes it plain that this Gallus was his kinsman and speaks feelingly of the slaughter at Perugia; that was his own country.

In spite of this declaration of no confidence, the second book is addressed to Maecenas, who knew a good poet when he saw one and must have exerted himself to win over this particular one. It is probably impossible to overstate the debt of the Augustan *régime* to the literary taste and genius for friendship of the complicated Maecenas. When, after his breach with Maecenas, Augustus took literary patronage into his own hands, the immediate result was the pressuring of Horace and apparently of Propertius, the more distant the banishment of Ovid, and the ultimate outcome several generations' silence.[1] If the Augustan *régime* cuts a good figure in great literature, one can hardly except as a reason the protection that Maecenas afforded his poets. He chose them with a taste that failed only, and failed signally, to correct his own writings, he gave them financial independence if they needed it, and he left them to follow their own bent. Virgil could profess that the *Georgics*, a labour of love if ever there was one, were the result of Maecenas' harsh commands (*tua, Maecenas, haud mollia iussa*), Horace and Propertius could pretend that Maecenas wanted them to celebrate Augustus' exploits, which they would have been delighted to do if their powers had permitted. But that was formal and conventional and everybody knew it. Virgil had set the pattern for his successors in the *Sixth Eclogue*, and with reference to a figure much less grand than that of the *princeps*. In the opening lines of that poem he took up and politicised a theme of Callimachus, which for its originator had only a literary import: Apollo forbade Callimachus to thunder in epic because Callimachus did not want to write epic; he told Virgil to stick to bucolic because Virgil did not want to celebrate the exploits of Alfenus Varus. Of course Octavian and Maecenas had more constraining power than Varus, but there is little to suggest

[1] Propertius may have been among those who early chose silence (below, p. 118).

that Maecenas was inclined to use it. The recurrence of the Callimachean apology is certainly in itself no evidence for pressure; the theme was as suitable for literary variation as other themes, culminating in Ovid's agreeable pretence that he had tried to write a *Gigantomachia* containing the *princeps'* praises but had found himself discontent with the result. Facts are more important, and the facts of these years of the twenties, if we contrast them with those that followed, show that poetry was not yet under pressure. In consequence, the *régime* was granted a glory that its ultimate tendency belied.

Even after Maecenas' fall the progress of suppression of opinion was not swift. Though Horace and Propertius both produced some poems to order, Ovid, socially *persona grata* and protected by powerful friends in the Roman aristocracy, wrote as he chose until his banishment. A crucial document here is his *apologia* to the *princeps* even after his exile (*Tristia* II). A *deprecatio irae* in traditional style, with many points of contact with Cicero's *pro Ligario*,[1] it is insinuating in its earlier section (uses indeed what the rhetorical treatises call *insinuatio*, a specially elaborate proem necessary when the mind of the judge is prejudiced against the speaker), but in its later arguments manly, direct and witty, and on the central issue of the poet's freedom uncompromising. That it did not succeed is true; but it is historically rather more important that a man so intelligent and eloquent as Ovid saw no reason why it should not. If Ovid, in the later years of Augustus' principate and after a deadly blow, could still speak out, we should certainly be wary of hypotheses that erect Offices of Propaganda in the twenties, and be prepared to find here too evidences that not all poets spoke with one voice.

Propertius' first use of the Callimachean apology occurs at once in 2.1. Love is his theme and his mistress his inspiration; if he could rise to epic he would not imitate Hesiod or Homer (the order of preference is Alexandrian), nor the historical epics of Choerilus, Ennius and (surprisingly to us) Cicero, but would sing instead of Caesar's exploits and of Maecenas. The list of exploits follows and is not in all respects a tactful one: we have the Sicilian

---

[1] The similarities were pointed out to me by Mr. A. F. Wallace-Hadrill.

war against Sextus Pompeius and the conquest of Egypt, both
respectable themes, but also the civil battles of Mutina and
Philippi and, most significantly for Propertius, 'the ruined hearths
of the ancient Etruscan race'. In the post-Actium years few cared
to remind the clement *princeps* of his bloody progress to Perugia.
More gracefully, Maecenas' loyalty is praised. But such high
subjects are not for the poet, who must stick to his last and who
has his own ideals (47 f.):

> *Laus in amore mori, laus altera si datur uno*
> *posse frui; fruar o solus amore meo.*

It is a glorious merit to die in love, a second glorious merit if the gods
grant enjoyment of one love; may I alone have the enjoyment of mine.

The extraordinary couplet has provoked controversy, though its
meaning seems clear; glorious merit (*laus*) is secured by virtuous
exertion, and there are two of them, persistence in love till death
and persistence in one love. There is also a third thing, a blessing,
not to be won by exertion, but a gift of god to be prayed for,
unchallenged enjoyment of that love. But the controversy has
distracted attention from what we should be feeling, which is
shock; one needs to imagine what Cicero's horrified exclamation
might have been ('*O hominem nequam!*'). For men *laus* belongs in
Roman tradition to the soldier and statesman; only a woman
could derive *laus* from the enjoyment of one love, and married
love at that, and many women proudly record on their tomb-
stones that they did so, were *univirae*. The inversion of roles has
its parallel elsewhere in Propertius;[1] here it is a deliberate affront
to received ideas and even more to the moral reformation that
Octavian in these years was trying to effect.[2] The praise of the

---

[1] The claim in his epitaph on himself (2.13.36) 'He was once the slave of a single
love' also recalls the female epitaphs. Cf. also his appropriation of Andromache's
words in 1.11.23 f., above, p. 56 n.1, and see further below, p. 152.

[2] The opposition from the fashionable classes that killed the attempted moral
legislation of (probably) 28 B.C. finds more explicit expression in 2.7, where
Propertius rejoices that it was not proceeded with, as it would have divided him
from Cynthia. 'How on earth should I provide children for Parthian triumphs?
There will be no soldier born of my seed. But if I could follow the real camp, that
of my mistress, Castor's horse would not be tall enough for me.' The persistent
princeps carried his legislation ten years later.

emperor's exploits is sandwiched between the opening description of Cynthia as Propertius' inspiration and the development of this astonishing couplet, in which he asserts at length and with variety of example his resolution to live and die in love. There is no reason to believe that Augustus's reaction to this scheme of values would have been much different from Cicero's. Maecenas is another matter. His magnificent figure appears again at the end of the poem, tying its two halves together; he is riding in a luxurious and fashionable British chariot,[1] urged to weep as he passes by the poet's grave and to say, 'A hard-hearted girl killed the poor wretch'; but the emperor has disappeared from view. No poem of the post-Actium years is so remarkable, none less a sign of a heart reconciled to the *régime*.

In other poems we have to consider the possibility that what we are being offered is mockery, and mockery not all that covert, of the new order. The hypothesis is sometimes ruled out on what seem purely *a priori* grounds, but there are cases where attention to the actual words the poet uses make it hard to exclude. In 2.10, perhaps another prefatory poem (see above, p. 41), he represents himself as eager, now that he has sung of his mistress, to put on a graver countenance, assume a more stately gait, and take up a grander instrument, Apollo's great concert *cithara*, mentioned only here in Propertius except for 4.6.69, where Apollo himself asks for it.[2] The purpose of all this parade is to enable him to sing the triumphs of the *princeps* (now Augustus); but he rapidly lets his enthusiasm decline into the wish that he may live to see the day when his ambition can be realised. In the rest of the book no events relevant to the *princeps* are mentioned except three that are more relevant to poetry, the opening of the portico attached to the temple of the Palatine Apollo (the portico housed the libraries of

---

[1] Maecenas is presented as himself; he chose to be thought not an official figure either. Recollections of Boadicea advancing to the sack of Camulodunum are not useful in fixing the significance of his British chariot. When Cicero in Cilicia met Vedius Pollio riding in a British chariot with a couple of pet baboons, he thought he had never seen a greater wastrel (*Att.* 6.1.25); and in the *Second Philippic* he exclaimed of Antony (58), 'He rode in a British chariot, he a tribune of the plebs!'

[2] *aliam citharam* means 'another instrument, the *cithara*'. Editors who translate it as 'another *cithara*' suggest that Propertius means the *barbiton*. But the instrument of Sappho and Anacreon is inappropriate for Propertius' purpose.

Greek and Latin literature), the inception of the *Aeneid*, and the death of Cornelius Gallus, cited as Propertius' exemplar and with no apologetic reference to his rashness in provoking the *princeps'* displeasure such as we find attached elsewhere to mention of him.

But 2.10, one might say, was no more, or anyway not much more, than the emperor heard from other poets, and perhaps we should not overstress Propertius' comic picture of himself in the posture of the grandiose bard. A poem from Book III is more surprising (3.4):

> *Arma deus Caesar dites meditatur ad Indos,*
> * et freta gemmiferi findere classe maris.*
> *magna, viri, merces. parat ultima terra triumphos;*
> * Tigris et Euphrates sub iuga vestra fluent.*
> *sera, sed Ausoniis veniet provincia virgis;* 5
> * assuescent Latio Partha tropaea Iovi.*
> *ite agite, expertae bello date lintea prorae,*
> * et solitum armigeri ducite munus equi.*
> *omina fausta cano. Crassos clademque piate.*
> * ite et Romanae consulite historiae.* 10
>
> *Mars pater et sacrae fatalia lumina Vestae,*
> * ante meos obitus sit precor illa dies,*
> *qua videam spoliis oneratos Caesaris axis,*
> * ad vulgi plausus saepe resistere equos,*
> *tela fugacis equi et bracati militis arcus,* 15
> * et subter captos arma sedere duces,*
> *inque sinu carae nixus spectare puellae*
> * incipiam et titulis oppida capta legam.*
> *ipsa tuam serva prolem, Venus; hoc sit in aevum*
> * cernis ab Aenea quod superesse caput.* 20
>
> *Praeda sit haec illis quorum meruere labores;*
> * me sat erit Sacra plaudere posse Via.*

1–10. The god Caesar is planning war against the rich Indians and an expedition over the pearl-bearing sea [the Persian Gulf]. Great is the profit, men. The ends of the earth are preparing triumphs; the Tigris and Euphrates will flow beneath your yoke. Though late, a province will be added to the Italian emblems of power; the trophies of Parthia will get used to the Latin Jove. Come now, you ships well-tried in war, spread your sails, do your usual duty and lead the way, you mail-clad horses. The omens I sing are propitious. Wipe out the stain of the Crassi and their disaster. Go off and do your best for Roman history.[1]

11–20. Father Mars and holy Vesta's light of destiny, let there be before my death, I beseech, that day on which I shall see Caesar's chariot loaded with spoils, his horses often coming to a stop at the mob's applause, the arrows of the horse in flight, the trousered soldier's bow, and the captive generals sitting under the weapons, and when, propped on my dear girl's lap, I shall gaze at the show and read the names of conquered cities on the notices. Preserve your own descendant, Venus; let this head, survivor as you see of Aeneas' line, live for ever.

21–2. Let this booty be theirs who have deserved it; I shall be content with applauding beside the Sacred Way.

Of the Augustan poets only Propertius and Ovid call Augustus a god outright. 'Gross and tactless flattery', one might say, but this is perhaps not so. After the dangerous early ventures of *Georgics* I and *Odes* 1.2, Virgil and Horace respected the emperor's caution, and speak of him as god's vice-gerent, or look forward to his future apotheosis; that was the correct line, and in the present poem especially the casual *deus Caesar* has a flavour of offensiveness, even apart from the antithesis lying in wait for it at the beginning of 3.5 (above, p. 81). So have some of the epithets and other terms: the Indians are rich, the Persian Gulf breeds pearls, the profit looks sizeable, Caesar's triumphal chariot will be laden with spoils, booty is the aim of the war. Good luck to those who want it; Propertius is not one. Anxious editors, having established that we must regard the ships and horses as addressed in the vocative case, assure us that of course we should not take them as the recipients of the grand imperatives of 9–10. Is that quite so certain? and if it is they who are told to go off and avenge Carrhae has the adjuration not overbalanced into absurdity? The solemn appeal to Rome's most ancient deities introduces the picture of the bustling triumph (the mob of course applauds); set against it is the picture of the very unbustling lover, watching the show in his mistress's embrace. The lover also has a deity to appeal to, and can

---

[1] The content of this cheerful phrase is less grandiose than its expression; it means simply, 'Give the historians something to write about.'

appropriately urge his own goddess Venus to preserve Augustus. The Julian line did of course boast of their descent from her, as Propertius points out, but this is perhaps an oddish moment to emphasise it; it was not the amatory aspect of Venus that was usually stressed when she was brought into association with the imperial line. It can hardly be the case that Augustus much liked this poem; he heard nothing like it from the loyal Horace.

This we can say, even though Propertius here apparently has his eye on a particular poem of Horace's, which equally contrasts the privacy of the poet with the cares of the governor of the world (*Carm.* 3.14):

> *Herculis ritu modo dictus, o plebs,*
> *morte venalem petiisse laurum,*
> *Caesar Hispana repetit penates*
> *   victor ab ora.*
> *unico gaudens mulier marito*   5
> *prodeat iustis operata sacris,*
> *et soror clari ducis et decorae*
> *   supplice vitta*
> *virginum matres iuvenumque nuper*
> *sospitum; vos, o pueri et puellae*   10
> *iam virum expertae, male inominatis*
> *   parcite verbis.*
>
> *Hic dies vere mihi festus atras*
> *exiget curas: ego nec tumultum*
> *nec mori per vim metuam tenente*   15
> *   Caesare terras.*
>
> *I pete unguentum, puer, et coronas*
> *et cadum Marsi memorem duelli*
> *Spartacum si qua potuit vagantem*
> *   fallere testa.*   20
> *dic et argutae properet Neaerae*
> *murreum nodo cohibere crinem.*
> *si per invisum mora ianitorem*
> *   fiet—abito.*
> *lenit albescens animos capillus*   25
> *litium et rixae cupidos protervae;*

non ego haec ferrem calidus iuventa
consule Planco.

1-12. He we were lately told, o commons, had like Hercules sought the bay whose price is death, Caesar is now coming back from the ends of Spain to his home. Let his wife, rejoicing in her unique husband, come forth and sacrifice duly, and our glorious leader's sister and, decked with suppliant ribbons, the mothers of maidens and of youths now lately saved; you lads, and lasses with a man already, speak no ill-omened words.

13-16. This day, truly a feast day to me, shall expel black cares: I shall fear neither riot nor death by violence while Caesar governs the world.

17-28. Go, lad, fetch perfume and garlands and a cask that remembers the Marsian war, if a pot was at all able to hide from the marauding Spartacus. And tell clear-voiced Neaera to hurry and do up her chestnut hair in a knot. If the hateful doorkeeper makes you wait—go off. Whitening hair makes mild the passions that crave quarrels and bullying fights; I should not have endured this in the heat of youth, in Plancus' consulship.

Horace here starts by addressing the people, as Propertius starts by addressing the army. He ends with the picture of himself preparing a private party to celebrate the public event, as Propertius imagines himself reclining in his mistress's arms during the triumph. But these similarities fade before the differences. Why is Horace not with Caesar? He is aging, aging too much even to care about Neaera if it will mean any fuss. The passions of youth that made him fight at Philippi *consule Planco* would also then have made him assault Neaera's closed doors; not now. Now he wants security from personal violence, and Caesar guarantees it. The war with the Italian allies, the uprising of the slaves under Spartacus (not events of Horace's lifetime, though he half suggests they were), these are no longer things to fear. The generation that lived through the civil wars has found a protector and can retire in peace to private life. The motives presented have nothing in common with those of Propertius:

Let this booty be theirs who have deserved it; I shall be content with applauding beside the Sacred Way.

Propertius is not and does not pretend to be middle-aged; he is in the prime of youth, and he does not care for plunder.

Moreover the private person Horace is not juxtaposed with the figure of the *princeps*, who does not in fact appear. What situation is envisaged as the occasion for the ode? Is Augustus going to enter the city on this *dies festus* or is the holiday a *supplicatio*, a feast of thanksgiving, decreed by the senate on receipt of the news that he was returning? We are not told, and this perhaps means that we should not enquire. The essential is that the person of the *princeps* is absent from the poem. We have no such clash between the triumphant general and the negligent lover as in Propertius.

Nothing, one would say, can turn Propertius' poem into a satisfactory eulogy of the Emperor. I suppose we might be told that Propertius has failed to appreciate Horace's subtle artistry, has read him so carelessly that all he has picked up is the possibility of conjoining the pictures of public rejoicing and private celebration, and has juxtaposed them ham-handedly, adding as well some flippant reflexions about the martial spirit's being prompted by love of gain such as Horace had in 1.29 addressed to the young Iccius but would never attach to the *princeps*. The total result would then indeed be offensive to the *princeps*, but quite unintentionally, the outcome of clumsiness merely. But if we were told this, why should we believe it rather than that the poet weighed his words and meant what he said, especially as he said it all over again at the beginning of the next poem?

> *Pacis Amor deus est, pacem veneramur amantes;*
> *stant mihi cum domina proelia dura mea.*
> *nec tamen inviso pectus mihi carpitur auro,*
> *nec bibit e gemma divite nostra sitis,*
> *nec mihi mille iugis Campania pinguis aratur,*
> *nec miser aera paro clade, Corinthe, tua.*

Peace has Love as its god, peace is what we lovers worship; my cruel persistent battles are with my mistress. And my heart does not hanker after gold, however envied (?),[1] nor my thirst drink from a rich gem,

---

[1] The sense here attributed to *invisus* seems unexampled, but no other sense is really compatible with *tamen*.

nor do a thousand teams plough fertile Campania for me, nor do I wretchedly amass bronzes by your destruction, Corinth.

That Propertius falls short of Horace's exquisite address in compliment is true, of course; but it is not so certain that he was here aiming at it.

Another poem that does end in a handsome panegyric of Augustus also shows the poet in a position of detachment from him (3.11). Propertius represents himself as surprised at the surprise of an anonymous critic, who blames his subjection to a woman and the consequent slothfulness of his life. He defends himself by heroic examples: Medea subjected Jason, Penthesilea Achilles, Omphale Hercules, Semiramis Jupiter himself (cf. *CQ* NS. 18, 1968, 317). All of them were Eastern queens and princesses, and so was a contemporary figure, Cleopatra, to whom Propertius proceeds to devote the greater part of his poem. The magnitude of the rescue effected by Actium is elaborately expressed and Augustus exalted; yet the starting point of the poem is the poet's inability to share any such heroic endeavours. It stands next to another in which his kinsman, the energetic Propertius Postumus, presumably at the beginning of the career that was to carry him so high, is reproached for following Augustus to war and deserting his charming wife. Desire for glory, greed for plunder, madness are the suggested motives:

> *Postume, plorantem potuisti linquere Gallam,*
> *miles et Augusti fortia signa sequi?*
> *tantine ulla fuit spoliati gloria Parthi,*
> *ne faceres Galla multa rogante tua?*
> *si fas est, omnes pariter pereatis avari,*
> *et quisquis fido praetulit arma toro.*
> *tu tamen iniecta tectus, vesane, lacerna*
> *potabis galea fessus Araxis aquam.*

Postumus, had you the heart to leave Galla weeping, and to follow Augustus' gallant standards as a soldier? Was any glory won from a despoiled Parthian worth it, when your Galla kept asking you not to do it? If I may pray so, may all you creatures of greed perish, and anyone who prefers warfare to a faithful bed! Yet you, you madman,

with your cloak wrapped round you, will wearily drink the water of
Araxes from your helmet.

Courage Postumus displays, no doubt; but he deserved a much
worse wife.

Of course the attitude is not individual or novel; few ancient
attitudes were. Well before Horace, Virgil too had contrasted
himself, 'flowering in the pursuits of inglorious ease' as he wrote
the *Georgics*, with Caesar thundering at the Euphrates and re-
organising the world. Yet in the elegists the praise of peace and
the easeful life has a political significance that it did not have in
the older poets. Their alienation mattered because they belonged
precisely to the class that Augustus wanted to involve. The
revolution had been made for their benefit if they would only
exert themselves to gather the glittering fruits it offered them.
Their refusal to do so, their mocking rejection of the true path of
honour and ambition, was a political offence, and felt as such,
punished when the due time came by the exactly calculated penalty
of Ovid's banishment to Tomi. Propertius was perhaps fortunate
in being some years older, and probably learnt caution a bit
earlier too.

In the light of this lack of commitment it is worth re-
examining a difficult and ambiguous poem (3.9), the central
statement in the book on Propertius' poetic aims. It is once more
addressed to Maecenas and is one of the few poems in the book to
have such an addressee (3.12 to Postumus and 3.22 to Tullus are
the only others). The first line presents Maecenas as an enigma,
eques Etrusco de sanguine regum, a Roman knight from the blood
of Etruscan kings, and the poem deploys again the Callimachean
apology in terms of this enigma. Maecenas is represented as
urging Propertius towards the vast sea of epic, for which his ship
is too small and where he would be in too much danger of disgraceful defeat. Different talents aim at different ends, win
different prizes. Even in the world of art we find differences, not
all internally determined; some are differences of scale and subject
matter, some are differences of expense. In other activities of life
too some differences are a matter of status, some of nature. But of
course there is also training, theoretical and practical (*praecepta*

and *exempla*), to reinforce circumstances and nature; and here Propertius' mentor is Maecenas. If circumstances and nature did not sufficiently direct him on the right path, the *vitae praecepta* and *exempla* of Maecenas would do so. Maecenas could pursue an official and military career and Caesar would give him power to achieve any design, but he has chosen retirement (*in tenuis humilem te colligis umbras*), shunning grandeur and the heat and dust of the day; though his boat is big enough, he has chosen not to let out his sail to the full. And by this judgement he wins no less glory than if he had aimed at a more impressive career. The repetition of the opening image of the ship has brought us back to the starting point, and the development of the poem to this point is revealed as an explication of its opening couplets.

The image continues, and is now re-applied to Propertius (35 ff.):

> *Non ego velifera tumidum mare findo carina;*
> *tota sub exiguo flumine nostra mora est.*
> *non flebo in cineres arcem sedisse paternos*
> *Cadmi nec semper proelia clade pari,*
> *nec referam Scaeas et Pergama, Apollinis arces,*
> *et Danaum decimo vere redisse ratis,*   40
> *moenia cum Graio Neptunia pressit aratro*
> *victor Palladiae ligneus artis equus.*
> *inter Callimachi sat erit placuisse libellos*
> *et cecinisse modis, Coe poeta, tuis.*
> *haec urant pueros, haec urant scripta puellas,*   45
> *meque deum clament et mihi sacra ferant.*

I am not cleaving the swelling sea in a ship sped by sail; my lingering is totally down by the tiny stream. I shall not bewail that Cadmus' citadel collapsed into the fathers' ashes and the battles that did not always end in equal ruin, nor tell of the Scaean gates and Pergama, Apollo's citadels, and how the Danaan ships returned in the tenth spring, when the victorious wooden horse of Pallas' devising drove a Greek plough over the walls Neptune built. It will be enough for me to have given pleasure among the books of Callimachus and to have sung in your strains, poet of Cos. May these be the writings that inflame lads and girls, and make them call me a god and sacrifice to me.

So far, probably so good. The Callimachean apology has issued, as we expect it to issue, in a rejection of epic, though, we may note, traditional heroic epic, not the celebration of contemporary themes but the war of the sons of the Seven against Thebes and topics of the *Iliad* and other poems of the Trojan cycle. The Callimachean topic, that is, is perhaps being reclaimed for Callimachean purposes, used to exclude a poetic genre, not, as commonly in Roman poetry, to exclude a particular subject matter. Callimachus and Philetas are to be Propertius' models and writings thus limited to be what wins him glory. We are not, it seems, told the subject matter of these writings. The reference to boys and girls does not authorise us to infer that Propertius is talking about love poetry. Perhaps the reverse, if we remember the opening of the third book of the *Odes*:

I hate and ban the unconsecrated mob; be silent all; songs not heard before as priest of the Muses I sing to maidens and boys.

As Williams remarks there, 'this choice of audience prepares the reader for a certain didactic element in the poetry'. Nor does 'inflame' necessarily imply love poetry; the flames of enthusiasm for fine poetry can burn as brightly as those of love. We probably have in fact the same conjunction of a reference to Callimachus and Philetas with an allusion to Horace as Propertius later employed at the opening of the Actium poem (4.6.1 ff.: see below, pp. 159ff.):

The bard is offering sacrifice; let all mouths be silent . . . Let a Roman writing-tablet vie with Philetas' ivy clusters and the urn pour the waters of Cyrene [Callimachus' home town] . . .

And the subject matter of that poem is of course not at all amatory.

What follows in 3.9, however, is puzzling: I offer a translation, but with the warning that in each case except the last 'I shall' could equally be 'I should', as the forms used are ambiguous. The certain futures are 'my talent will grow' and 'I shall be said'.

Te duce vel Iovis arma canam caeloque minantem
Coeum et Phlegraeis Oromedonta iugis;

celsaque Romanis decerpta Palatia tauris
  ordiar et caeso moenia firma Remo,   50
eductosque pares silvestri ex ubere reges,
  crescet et ingenium sub tua iussa meum.
prosequar et currus utroque ab litore ovantis,
  Parthorum astutae tela remissa fugae,
castraque Pelusi Romano subruta ferro,   55
  Antonique gravis in sua fata manus.
mollia tu coeptae fautor cape lora iuventae,
  dexteraque immissis da mihi signa rotis.
hoc mihi, Maecenas, laudis concedis, et a te est
  quod ferar in partis ipse fuisse tuas.   60

With you leading the way I shall sing even of the warfare of Jove, and of Coeus threatening heaven and of Oromedon on the hills of Phlegra; and I shall set about telling of the lofty Palatine's being cropped by Roman bulls and the walls secured by Remus' murder, and of the twin kings reared by the teats of the woodland creature, and my talent will grow to meet your commands. I shall escort too the chariots triumphant over east and western shores, the arrows the Parthians hurl back in cunning flight, Pelusium's fortress destroyed by Roman steel, Antony's hands cruel to his own destruction. Gentle be your touch on the reins as you back my youth now making a beginning, and favourable the applause you give me as my wheels start racing. This merit you grant me, Maecenas, and it is because of you that I, even I, shall be said to have been on your side.

It is not altogether easy to see what is being said, and the couplet that causes the trouble is the first one. The war of the gods and giants is a Hesiodic theme, not a Homeric one; *a priori* then, it might seem not excluded by an Alexandrian ideal of poetry. But Propertius does specifically rule it out as un-Callimachean at 2.1.39 f.:

Sed neque Phlegraeos Iovis Enceladique tumultus
  intonet angusto pectore Callimachus.

But Callimachus would not thunder from his narrow breast the riot of Jove and Enceladus at Phlegra.

It is hard not to believe that that determines the meaning of the couplet here, that is, that Propertius is taking the idea of his writing of the gods and giants as absurd. This suggests then that the first phrase means, 'If (as you won't) you lead the way by changing your manner of life, I should sing . . .' If the lines that follow are to carry on this unreal conditional, one must alter *crescet* to *crescat* ('my talent would grow') and one must also assume that these lines describe an enterprise equally impossible for a Callimachean Propertius. But do they? Take the very first of them, 'the lofty Palatine's being cropped by Roman bulls', and turn to the opening lines of Book IV:

> *Hoc quodcumque vides, hospes, qua maxima Roma est,*
> *ante Phrygem Aenean collis et herba fuit;*
> *atque ubi Navali stant sacra Palatia Phoebo*
> *Evandri profugae procubuere boves.*

Whatever you see here, stranger, where majestic Rome stands, before Phrygian Aeneas was a hill and grass; and where the Palatine rises, holy to Phoebus of the Ships, Evander's roaming oxen came to rest.

The murder of Remus is not impossible for elegy (Ovid was to prove it) and certainly not the nurture of the twins. Even if we leave 4.6 out of account as a poem that in its present form is certainly later, Augustus' war with Antony is so far from being an impossible topic that two poems further on, at the central point of the book, Propertius offered a forty-line development on the victory over Cleopatra. For the purposes of this book that development is rather uneasily accommodated to the form of love elegy. But it, or something like it, could figure in a grander design.

More important, if we take this whole passage to describe an enterprise that Propertius is not going to embark on, it is difficult to make it cohere with the last lines of the poem, the section beginning, 'Gentle be your touch . . .' What is the task on which Propertius' youth is making a beginning? Surely not love elegy, which he had been writing for years. That it is love elegy is the assumption of those editors who remove the lines from 'With you leading the way . . .' to '. . . cruel to his own destruction' and either intrude them into the tightly knit context in which Propertius passes from the promptings of nature to the training offered by

Maecenas' example or remove them to the end, where they hang as an unpersuasive pendant.

Moreover, the removal of the lines disrupts a delicately allusive context. When we hear 'and my talent will grow to meet your commands' (*crescet et ingenium sub tua iussa meum*) and a few lines later 'Gentle be your touch on the reins as you back my youth now making a beginning' (*mollia tu coeptae fautor cape lora iuventae*), it is not irrelevant to recall that both Propertius and Maecenas knew the *Georgics* rather well. Virgil in Book II uses the images both of the ship and of the car (39 ff. 'Be present to aid and run to shore with me on the task I have begun, ... Maecenas, and speeding give me full sails over an open sea', 541 f. 'But we have completed a measureless surface lap by lap and by now it is time to unyoke my horses' steaming necks'). In Book III, recalling himself from the promise of a poem of epic stature in praise of Caesar, one in which he will bring the Muses down from the peak of Helicon, he returns (40 ff.) to dealing with the Dryads' woods and inviolate glades, *tua, Maecenas, haud mollia iussa*; the inviolate glades, *intacti saltus*, remind us of Callimachus' untrodden way, the ungentle command to follow it is that of Maecenas, without whose aid, Virgil goes on, his mind can conceive and forward no high project (*te sine nil altum mens incohat*). In Book II Propertius had twice spoken of himself as still fixed at the stage, *mutatis mutandis*, of the *Eclogues*, in 2.10.25 f. (perhaps the opening poem of a book, see above, p. 41):

My songs do not yet know the springs of Ascra, but Love has bathed them only in Permessus' stream,

and, more elaborately, in the last poem of the book (2.34.61 ff.). By the end of 3.9[1] he seems to be professing readiness to accept Maecenas' suasion to a higher task, not epic, which has already been excluded in lines 37 ff., but the Roman *Aetia*, still elegiac and

---

[1] It is not easy to decide whether the couplet 47 f. (above, p. 112) represents an incoherence in the poet's thought or suggests that the text is at this point lacunose. Certainly, one does not expect to find, 'I should do even x' and 'I shall do y' linked by the particle -*que*. If Propertius did so link them, it perhaps indicates something muffled and oblique in his attitude to the new task.

Callimachean, but different from his poetry hitherto, more serious, more Roman, more in harmony with the professed ideals of the *régime*. If this is so, the last couplet too makes sense, though unexpected sense; it is Maecenas' tact and understanding that have done the work of reconciliation and the faction that after ages will say Propertius adhered to is that of Maecenas, not Caesar. It may be that we find this interpretation (the obvious meaning of the words) hard to arrive at and make sense of only because no other Augustan poet showed a similar wary truthfulness.

Whether for the reason that he here suggests or not, Propertius even in this book offered a specimen laudation of Augustus' achievement (3.11), and it seems certain that he embarked on the *Aetia*, but never got far with it. The real problem turned out in the end to be not subject matter but style. Themes of early Roman history, pastoral or significant of more than themselves, the picturesque and pathetic elements of the contemporary scene, these were topics that a great poet, even one with a less than total commitment to the *status quo*, could make a great poem of; what Propertius did not solve was the question of how.

CHAPTER FOUR

Propertius' Last Book

A LONGISH interval separates Book IV from the earlier ones. Not many of the individual poems are dateable, even in their present form, and some may have been subject to retouching; three (1, 6, 11) allude to events of 16 B.C., while 3 has a dramatic date perhaps not later than the settlement with Parthia in 20 B.C. (of course this would not in any case tell us the date of composition). None of the others gives any clue. Poem 7 speaks of Cynthia as dead; this might be true. Sentimental editors tend to think that the other Cynthia poem (8), a comic masterpiece, must therefore be earlier, and generally put 5, the poem on the tempting procuress, back with it, on the ground that it too has attachments to love elegy (as in Ovid, *Amores* 1.8). The argument runs: 'Relations with Cynthia were finished in Book III and she is not mentioned in IV, except, as dead, in 4.7; therefore 4.8 does not belong to this period'; this is visibly unpersuasive. There are, we shall see, good reasons for regarding 4.7 and 4.8 as companion pieces (below, pp. 152 ff.). The other four poems of the book (2, 4, 9, 10) belong together, in that they could all be fragments of a projected Roman *Aetia*, an explanation of his nature by the god Vertumnus, whose statue stood at the entry to the Vicus Tuscus, the legend of Tarpeia who in the reign of Romulus betrayed the citadel to the Sabines (given as an explanation of the name of the Tarpeian Hill), a cheerful story explaining why women were excluded from the rites to Hercules at the Ara Maxima, and an account of the temple of Juppiter Feretrius and the three achievements that were kept in it of the *spolia opima*, the arms stripped from an enemy general by a Roman general who had killed him in personal combat. These four aetiological poems might be comparatively early, especially if it is right to see in 3.9 the promise of writing a Roman *Aetia*. The same is probably true of the first part of 4.1, which contains the prayer that the poet may become the Roman Callimachus and claims to be the preface to a poem on Rome's 'rites and calendar and the archaic names of places' (4.1.69 f.). 4.6, which seems to be promised in 3.9, may also largely belong here (below, p. 135).

It is perhaps most likely that one should look for the motive for the appearance of the book in the two honorific poems 4.6 and 4.11. The former has an occasion for publication that we can be fairly sure of, the quadriennial festival celebrating Augustus' rule that was held by Agrippa during the emperor's absence in 16 B.C. (Dio 54.19.8). The latter is an *epicedion* for a noble Roman matron, Cornelia, who died in the consulship of her brother in 16 B.C.; her paternal nobility was dazzling, but much is also made of her mother Scribonia, for a brief time Octavian's wife, and of the emperor's personal grief. As with the fourth book of Horace's *Odes*, it is hard to doubt that these elegies are ultimately commissioned works, and it seems likely that the poet built the book round them, using some materials he had to hand, recasting others, and probably writing some new poems. If this is right we can be grateful to the *princeps* for the creation or preservation of the book's three great poems, 4.3, 4.7 and 4.8.

This hypothesis assumes that the book was published by the poet himself, and made up with some difficulty after a period in which Propertius had not written much. Some have refused to believe this, particularly because of distaste for the juxtaposition of 4.7 and 4.8. Not all are as hysterical as Postgate, but his comment will serve as a specimen (*Select Elegies*, p. lv):

If viii had preceded vii, the contrast would have been startling enough. To pass thus from this warm-blooded lighthearted life in all its thoughtless bustle and enjoyment to the chill and shadowy ghost-land would, we may say without rashness, have been too violent a change for the Greek and too bold a one for the Roman. But to reverse the order and to bid nature revolve upon her track is a ghastly imagination, or rather Mephistophelian mockery, only possible to ages which have learnt to finger the secret springs of the horrible and produced the paintings of a Wiertz and the fiction of a Poe.

Propertius was admittedly not in the least like Poe; but the argument of impropriety neglects the fact that he was not like any

other nineteenth-century romantic, either. The collocation of the
two poems is to be explained on literary grounds, not sentimental
ones, and there is good reason for attributing it to Propertius
himself.

There is no reason either to accept the implicit assumption of
other editors that a poet goes on writing till he drops, and that as
the latest events mentioned by Propertius belong to 16 B.C. he
must have died soon after, leaving scraps of poems to be put
together by a friend. Yet in 16 B.C. the poet was probably only in
his mid-thirties or a little younger; he seems to have left descendants, unlike Horace he need not feel obliged to write, and much
goes to show that he did not share Ovid's Ciceronian inability to
hold his tongue. Gallus before him seems to have stopped being
a poet ten years or so before he died. If in particular Propertius
had attempted an *Aetia* and found it unworkable, he may have
been in an impasse, or indeed simply have got bored, or married,
or engaged in the business of managing an estate. The countrymen
of Congreve, at any rate, should be able to remember that even
great genius will not necessarily keep a gentleman in comfortable
circumstances perpetually scribbling away.

Though much about the genesis of the book is uncertain, it is
probably not misleading to consider first the group of aetiological
poems, and what the requirements of the genre were, and to
postpone for the moment the discussion of elegies that were either
certainly or probably written or rewritten later.

There was nothing particularly novel in the idea of employing
the aetiological technique on Roman legend. Indeed Callimachus
himself had included two Roman stories in the *Aetia*, the reproach
of his mother to a limping Gaius (fr. 106) and an explanation of
some features of the cult of Diana Nemorensis (fr. 190, where
Pfeiffer's note is very informative). Roman historical epic was of
course from the beginning concerned with 'origins' and Ennius
had told of the sports at the dedication of the temple of Juppiter
Feretrius, the subject of Propertius 4.10 (*Ann.* 1 fr. LI). Much in
the Roman historiographic tradition about ancient times was
built up from such attempts to explain present customs; the first
book of Livy is full of examples, and so are the Italian books of

the *Aeneid*. The great antiquarian scholar, M. Terentius Varro, whose long and useful life extended to 27 B.C., himself wrote a work called *Aetia* explaining customs of Roman private life, notably marriage customs. In the report of one of these explanations (of why people shake hands with the right hand) he is said to have 'followed Callimachus'; the phrasing perhaps suggests agreement with Callimachus in detail, not mere imitation of his title (Callimachus, fr. 189). The fragments of Varro's *Aetia* are not cited verbatim, and though they look prosy enough, we cannot exclude the possibility that they were in verse, and that this was why he chose the title *Aetia* to distinguish this work from other of his antiquarian writings which of course involved aetiology. But we know enough of Varro's style in both prose and verse to be sure that he could be no kind of stylistic help to a poet aiming to dazzle the Augustan age.

Two Greek authors of uncertain date also demand consideration. One of them, Simylus, is cited in Plutarch's life of Romulus (17.5) for the legend of Tarpeia, the subject of Propertius 4.4, and Plutarch quotes four elegiac couplets from the account. As in Propertius (though not in the rest of the tradition), Tarpeia's motive for her treachery is love for the opposing general and one could do with knowing whether Simylus anticipated Propertius in this. The theme is a Hellenistic one, especially in the legend in which Scylla betrayed her father Nisus for love of Minos. The latter story was something of a *cause célèbre* in Augustan literature. Gallus had perhaps alluded to it, as Virgil did in the *Eclogues* (6.74 ff.). Virgil at least confused Scylla daughter of Nisus with the Scylla of the *Odyssey*; the anonymous author of the *Ciris* took him to task (some time after the publication of the *Aeneid*) and retold the story of Scylla daughter of Nisus. Propertius himself had used the right Scylla as an example in 3.19.21 ff., and it would not be surprising if, in a Hellenistic mood, he had exploited her story to give an erotic direction to the legend of Tarpeia's betrayal. We could, that is, easily see Propertius as innovating in obedience to Alexandrian canons, rewriting a sordid legend in which Tarpeia's motive was merely greed for gold (according to the historians she bargained for the bracelets the Sabines wore on their left arms), and giving it a romantic interpretation by making her fall in love with the Sabine king Tatius as Scylla had done with Minos.

It is not clear, however, that the love interest had not been already introduced by Simylus. Simylus' story is eccentric, and in a way that may indicate that some elements of it belong to an older stratum than anything in the Roman tradition: his Tarpeia belongs not to the reign of Romulus in the eighth century but to the sack of Rome by the Gauls about 390 B.C. She was in love not with Tatius but with the Gallic chieftain Brennus. This has an analogy in Hellenistic erotic fiction: a later Brennus, the leader of the Gaulish invasion of Greece in the third century B.C., is brought into romantic association with a girl who betrayed Ephesus to him and who agreed to become his mistress if he gave her the gold his soldiers wore. The story is attributed to Clitophon of Rhodes, and in it as in Simylus the motives of love and gain are unconvincingly mingled; the gold ornaments of the soldiers seem more persuasive motives than the love. It arouses some unease, however, that such gold ornaments are traditionally also more appropriate to Gauls than to the primitive Sabines who wear them in the standard Roman legend;[1] moreover, a constant element in the story, that what Tarpeia betrayed was the *Capitol*, also better suits the period of the Gallic invasion, as the Capitol was no part of Romulus' city. So once more, it would not be surprising if in its origin the story was about a bargain for Gaulish gold, if an erotic motif sometimes got attached to it, if it entered Roman historiography as a legend about the Gaulish sack, but was decanted backwards in time (already, apparently, by Fabius Pictor in the third century B.C.) because of the multiplicity of other legends attaching to that sack, and particularly because of the steady Roman insistence that the Capitol was not in fact taken by the Gauls. In that case Simylus would represent an earlier stage of the tradition than Propertius or indeed than Fabius; that

---

[1] Archaeological assurances that in the fifth century B.C. some Italian peoples (not notably Sabines) did wear gold bracelets on their left arms really do nothing to illuminate investigation of an adulterated fiction like the Tarpeia story. What matters is the conventional picture of such peoples, and Sabines are conventionally frugal.

does not of course prove that he wrote earlier and perhaps does not even create a *prima facie* presumption that he did. But it seems something that needs explaining.

The other Greek poet we know of is Butas, who is said by Plutarch, again in the life of Romulus (21.6), to have written 'mythical *aetiae* about Roman affairs'; Plutarch, quoting one elegiac couplet, derives from him a story about the origin of the Lupercalia, while the Christian writer Arnobius cites him for an explanation of the presence of a wine jar and the absence of myrtle in the rites of the Bona Dea. Butas' name is the Doric equivalent of Butes or Bootes and means 'neatherd'; it is rare in real life and some have identified Butas the poet with the other historical Butas known to us, the freedman of Cato who witnessed his last days at Utica in 46 B.C. If the identification were right we should have a rather older contemporary of Propertius writing Roman *Aetia* in Greek before Propertius is likely to have done so in Latin; but it must be admitted that only the rarity of the name supports the identification.

In any case, the balance of evidence rather suggests that it was not an altogether novel enterprise when Propertius embarked on the task of writing Roman *Aetia* in elegiac verse. Becoming the Roman Callimachus was a different and more ambitious project. What was required beyond antiquarian learning was a framework, a style and a point of view. It was the last that was the most difficult, as we can see if we think back from Ovid's achievement in the *Fasti*. The learned Varro might expect few readers for the vast repositories of knowledge and conjecture that he produced in the 41 books of the *Antiquitates* and the 25 books of the *De Lingua Latina*, with their accompanying flotillas of monographs. Poets did want readers, and could not assume their good will. But if a work on antiquarian subject matter was not to be a bore poetically, a delicate and relentless presentation of a modern view-point had to be maintained, avoiding the pedantry of prose antiquarianism, but gracefully sidestepping as well the facetious and the solemn, faults of modernity. Novelty of idea, variety in presentation, eloquence pathetic or humorous, a narrative line flexible enough to tell a story in twenty lines or two hundred, a keen and interested eye for the relics of the past to be seen in the present, a stance that was nevertheless disengaged and casual, all these were essentials. There was probably no single Latin poem so hard to get right as the *Fasti*, no poet but Ovid who could have achieved it. In such a work it is largely continuity of flow that is engaging and to give a sample is in some respects misleading. But at any rate one can attempt a specimen of the requisite attitude and of the requisite style, with its harmonious mixture of learning poetical and antiquarian, its ease of movement and ingenuity of thought. The problem Ovid faced in this passage was how to make interesting to a cultivated and urban audience the unpromising subject of the festival of the goddess Robigo, who produced rust in wheat (*Fasti* 4.901 ff.):

> *Sex ubi quae restant luces Aprilis habebit,*
> *in medio cursu tempora veris erunt,*
> *et frustra pecudem quaeres Athamantidos Helles,*
> *signaque dant imbres exoriturque Canis.*
> *hac mihi Nomento Romam cum luce redirem,* 905
> *obstitit in media candida turba via;*
> *flamen in antiquae lucum Robiginis ibat,*
> *exta canis flammis, exta daturus ovis.*
> *protinus accessi ritus ne nescius essem;*
> *edidit haec flamen verba, Quirine, tuus:* 910
>
> *'Aspera Robigo, parcas Cerialibus herbis,*
> *et tremat in summa leve cacumen humo.*
> *tu sata sideribus caeli nutrita secundi*
> *crescere dum fiant falcibus apta sinas.*
> *vis tua non levis est: quae tu frumenta notasti* 915
> *maestus in amissis illa colonus habet.*
> *nec venti tantum Cereri nocuere nec imbres,*
> *nec sic marmoreo pallet adusta gelu,*
> *quantum si culmos Titan incalfacit udos.*
> *tunc locus est irae, diva timenda, tuae.* 920
> *parce, precor, scabrasque manus a messibus aufer,*
> *neve noce cultis. posse nocere sat est.*
> *nec teneras segetes, sed durum amplectere ferrum,*
> *quodque potest alios perdere, perde prior.*
> *utilius gladios et tela nocentia carpes;* 925

nil opus est illis: otia mundus agit.
sarcula nunc durusque bidens et vomer aduncus,
  ruris opes, niteant, inquinet arma situs,
conatusque aliquis vagina ducere ferrum
  adstrictum longa sentiat esse mora. 930
at tu ne viola Cererem, semperque colonus
  absenti possit solvere vota tibi.'

Dixerat; a dextra villis mantele solutis
  cumque meri patera turis acerra fuit.
tura focis vinumque dedi. ¿brasque bidentis 935
  turpiaque obscenae (vidimus) exta canis.
tum mihi 'Cur detur sacris nova victima quaeris?'
  (quaesieram) 'causam percipe', flamen ait.
'est Canis (Icarium dicunt) quo sidere moto
  tosta sitit tellus praecipiturque seges. 940
pro cane sidereo canis hic imponitur arae,
  et quare fiat nil nisi nomen habet.'

When April has six days left over, the season of spring will have run half its course and you will look in vain for Helle's beast [Aries], and the signs suggest rain and the Dog star rises. On this day when I was returning from Nomentum to Rome, my way was barred by a white-clad crowd on the high road; a *flamen* was making his way to the grove of ancient Robigo to give the fire the entrails of a dog and of a sheep. I at once drew near so as not to miss learning about the rite; these were the words, uttered by your *flamen*, Quirinus:

'Rough Robigo, spare Ceres' plants and let the top shoots be smooth as they flutter just above the ground. Allow the seedlings to grow under the influence of favourable weather until they are ready for the sickles. Your might is grievous: any wheat you have marked the mourning farmer counts as lost. Winds do not do so much harm to Ceres, nor rains, her colour is not so unhealthy when scorched by marble frost, as when the Titan god warms damp stalks. That gives a chance to your wrath, fearful goddess. Refrain, I beseech, and keep your scabby hands from the harvest, do not damage the tended fields! The power to harm is enough. Leave tender crops, embrace hard iron; it can destroy others, destroy it first. You will do better to seize on swords and dangerous arrows; they are not needed: the universe is at peace. Hoes now and the hard mattock and beaked ploughshare, the wealth of the countryside, let them shine, while weapons grow dirty with mould, and let someone

who tries to draw his blade from the sheath find it held hard by long
idleness. But do not violate Ceres, and let the farmer always be able to
pay his vows to you, but in your absence.'

He stopped; on his right was a napkin with loose nap, a dish of
unmixed wine, and a censer. He gave the fire the incense and wine, the
sheep's liver and (I saw it) the foul entrails of an unholy bitch. Then
he said to me, 'Why this strange victim? you ask' (I had asked). 'This
is the reason. There is a Dog (they call him Icarius), a constellation at
whose rising the scorched earth is thirsty and the crop ripens too soon.
Instead of the dog of the heavens this dog is put on the altar, and its
name is the only reason for its sacrifice.'

Such a passage as this can the better function as a specimen
because it deals with an episode that it is hard to make shine.
There is no entertaining legend, no brilliant procession to help the
poet along, but a simple rite of Roman agrarian cult. Its presentation is unified by the skilfully planted and astronomically quite
false reference to the Dog star's rising (it in fact had its apparent
setting a few days later than 25 April). But such astronomical
indications, though frequently inexact, are not always so func-
tional in the narrative of the *Fasti* as here, and the reader whose
astronomy is at all shaky is likely to pass it over. Our attention
anyway is at once distracted by the picture of the journeying poet,
of the traffic problem created by the crowd in holiday clothes, of
the *flamen* making his way to the grove; the result is that we miss
the point of the first reference to the sacrifice of a dog, so that the
flamen's final explanation still comes pat with a satisfying surprise.
The presence of the poet, innocently eager for instruction, informs
the whole scene and we see things through his eyes: even from a
distance through the crowd he can tell that the officiating priest is
a *flamen* (the olive-wood peak on his cap would indicate that), but
it is only when he draws near that he can identify him as the *flamen
Quirinalis*. But the pose of open-eyed curiosity is deceptive:
instead of describing the rite he professes himself so anxious not
to miss, the poet presents us first with a sophisticated hymn and
prayer that uses the conventional suggestion of an alternative
victim (here iron) to link the celebration of Robigo's power with
the theme, more interesting to contemporary readers, of universal

peace. The whole prayer is no very faithful rendering of Roman cult formulae; one could not spoil a modern poem by any near approach to those. The truth of the *flamen*'s final statement is elegantly underlined, to the horror of historians of religion who know that the Romans were fussy about such matters, by the fact that even the victim's gender is first indeterminate, then female, then male; that it is called *canis* is enough. The *Fasti* have many passages more brilliant and more moving, but this unassertive sleight of hand is dominant throughout the poem, and it is what keeps the reader in a permanent state of alert.

The framework Ovid chose was the uninhibiting one of the Roman calendar. Though it recommended twelve books, its diversity forbade the erection of imposing architectural schemes, but it forbade little else. The poet could at will be present or absent, could concentrate on the day's rite or on the legend invoked to explain it, could vary the scale of treatment to suit his own and his readers' taste. In the hands of some poets, for instance, the fatal day of the Ides of March could have produced hundreds of lines of tedious rhetoric on Caesar's murder. Ovid had a different story to tell, an ingenious and poetical combination of his own. The Ides of March were also the festival of the goddess Anna Perenna, a sort of public picnic by the Tiber which he affectionately describes; but he had more to tell about Anna Perenna than anyone had ever told before. Her identification, perhaps pre-existent, with Dido's sister enabled him to continue the story of *Aeneid IV* in a free invention of new and pathetic details. After the elaborate and sparkling novelty of this long section, Caesar's murder comes in for a dozen lines, startling at the outset, though flatteringly retrieved:

> *Praeteriturus eram gladios in principe fixos,*
> *cum sic a castis Vesta locuta focis:*
> *'Ne dubita meminisse. meus fuit ille sacerdos,*
> *sacrilegae telis me petiere manus.*   700
> *ipsa virum rapui simulacraque nuda reliqui;*
> *quae cecidit ferro, Caesaris umbra fuit'.*
> *ille quidem caelo positus Iovis atria vidit*
> *et tenet in magno templa dicata foro,*

et quicumque nefas ausi prohibente deorum
numine polluerant pontificale caput,
morte iacent merita. testes estote, Philippi,
et quorum sparsis ossibus albet humus.
hoc opus, haec pietas, haec prima elementa fuerunt
Caesaris, ulcisci iusta per arma patrem.

I was meaning to pass over the swords stuck in the *princeps*, when Vesta spoke from her chaste hearth: 'Do not hesitate to recall it. He was *my* priest, *I* was the target of the weapons in those sacrilegious hands. I myself snatched the hero away and left a bare image; what fell by the steel was Caesar's shade.' It is true he is set in heaven and has seen Jove's halls and has a temple to his name in the great Forum, and all those who ventured on the crime against the gods' will and polluted a pontiff's head, lie prostrate in well-deserved death. Bear witness, Philippi, and those whose scattered bones whiten the ground. This was the task, this the loving duty, this the ABC of Caesar, to avenge his father in justified war.

'Rites and the calendar and the ancient names of places' were what Propertius promised as the subject of his poem in 4.1.69. In the extant poems in Book IV rites and the ancient names of places are involved, only the former in the account of Hercules' irruption into the festival of the Bona Dea, only the latter in the Tarpeia poem, while those on the Vertumnus statue and the temple of Juppiter Feretrius have elements of both ritual and topographic significance. At the beginning of the book someone, presumably the poet, is pointing out to an unidentified *hospes*, the convenient 'stranger' of many inscriptional poems, sights of the modern city which he contrasts with their imagined past state (see above, p. 113); this leads, naturally enough, into a parallel contrast (21 ff.) between the exotic rites of the present day religious and the rustic cults of primitive Rome when

Vesta coronatis pauper gaudebat asellis,
ducebant macrae vilia sacra boves,
parva saginati lustrabant compita porci,
pastor et ad calamos exta litabat ovis.

Vesta was poor and took pleasure in garlanded asses, skinny cows drew carts with cheap ritual objects, the tiny crossroad shrines were purified by the sacrifice of fatted pigs and the shepherd successfully offered a sheep's entrails to the strains of a pipe.

Again we have the combination of topography and ritual. The fiction of the stranger being shown the sights of Rome is not maintained elsewhere, and the four poems deploy a variety of technique. In two the poet announces his intention of telling the tale (4.4.1 f., 4.10.1):

> *Tarpeium nemus et Tarpeiae turpe sepulcrum*
> *fabor et antiqui limina capta Iovis.*

> *Nunc Iovis incipiam causas aperire Feretri . . .*

I shall tell of the Tarpeian grove and Tarpeia's disgraceful burial and the capture of ancient Jove's home.

Now I shall begin to reveal the explanation of Juppiter Feretrius . . .

In 9 the manuscripts represent him as plunging straight into the story of Hercules' visit, though a prayer for Hercules' blessing on his book comes, out of place, just before the last couplet; scholars move the prayer either to the beginning or to the end of the poem (the former gives a neater result). In 2 the figure of the poet is not explicitly present and Vertumnus himself addresses someone who is surprised at his multiplicity of shapes and who is later said to be in a hurry to get to court as he has litigation on foot; the hurry is of course designed to enable Vertumnus to cut a long story short towards the end of the poem.

In the Vertumnus poem the point of view is naturally that of the present; the god stands in the Vicus Tuscus, well pleased with his situation (5 f.):

> *Haec me turba iuvat, nec templo laetor eburno;*
> *Romanum satis est posse videre Forum.*

I like this crowd and I don't joy in a temple of ivory; it is enough to be able to see the Roman forum.

He has his memories of the past, that he came from Vulsinii, that he once wore armour and was admired in it, that he saw the battle in the Forum between Romulus and Tatius, that in Romulus' reign he was made of maple wood until cast in metal by Mamurrius; other things are beyond even his memory, but he has heard of them (7 f.):

> *Hac quondam Tiberinus iter faciebat, et aiunt*
> *remorum auditos per vada pulsa sonos.*

Tiber used to make its way hereabouts, and they say the sound of oars was heard over the shallows they struck.

But what principally occupies him is his continuing ability to take on different forms, and most of his speech complacently describes what a Roman of the Augustan age could see. In the narrative poems, modernity depends on other features, the contrast between the urban present and the rustic city or open hills of old, the psychology that enables Tarpeia to analyse her passion with Alexandrian finesse, defending it by the examples of Scylla (the wrong one) and Ariadne, the intervention of the poet's own *persona* in apostrophe or comment.

The poem that best shows Propertius' stance here is 4.10, not the best of the aetiological poems, but the one at which he probably had to work hardest. The person of Vertumnus, the erotic pathos of Tarpeia, the lighthearted teasing of a discomfited Hercules, accommodated themselves easily to the modern world of elegy; the three achievements of the *spolia opima* were inescapably martial and, as it happened, inescapably archaic. More persistence was needed to fit them to the elegiac mode of speaking:

> *Nunc Iovis incipiam causas aperire Feretri*
> *armaque de ducibus trina recepta tribus.*
> *magnum iter ascendo, sed dat mihi gloria vires;*
> *non iuvat e facili lecta corona iugo.*
>
> *Imbuis exemplum primae tu, Romule, palmae*   5
> *huius, et exuvio plenus ab hoste redis,*
> *tempore quo portas Caeninum Acrona petentem*
> *victor in eversum cuspide fundis equum.*
> *Acron Herculeus Caenina ductor ab arce,*
> *Roma, tuis quondàm finibus horror erat.*   10
> *hic spolia ex umeris ausus sperare Quirini*

ipse dedit, sed non sanguine sicca suo.
hunc videt ante cavas librantem spicula turris
  Romulus et votis occupat ante ratis:
'Iuppiter, haec hodie tibi victima corruet Acron'. 15
  voverat, et spolium corruit ille Iovi.

Vrbis Virtutisque parens sic vincere suevit,
  qui tulit a parco frigida castra lare.
idem eques et frenis, idem fuit aptus aratris,
  nec galea hirsuta compta lupina iuba, 20
picta neque inducto fulgebat parma pyropo;
  praebebant caesi baltea lenta boves.

Cossus at insequitur Veientis caede Tolumni,
  vincere cum Veios posse laboris erat.
necdum ultra Tiberim belli sonus, ultima praeda 25
  Nomentum et captae iugera terna Corae.
heu Vei veteres, et vos tum regna fuistis,
  et vestro posita est aurea sella foro;
nunc intra muros pastoris bucina lenti
  cantat, et in vestris ossibus arva metunt. 30

Forte super portae dux Veiens astitit arcem,
  colloquiumque sua fretus ab urbe dedit.
dumque aries murum cornu pulsabat aeno,
  vinea qua ductum longa tegebat opus,
Cossus ait, 'Forti melius concurrere campo'. 35
  nec mora fit, plano sistit uterque gradum.
di Latias iuvere manus, desecta Tolumni
  cervix Romanos sanguine lavit equos.

Claudius at Rheno traiectos arcuit hostis,
  Belgica cum vasti parma relata ducis 40
Virdomari. genus hic Brenno iactabat ab ipso,
  nobilis e rectis fundere gaesa rotis.
illi virgatas maculanti sanguine bracas
  torquis ab incisa decidit unca gula.

Nunc spolia in templo tria condita; causa Feretri 45
  omine quod certo dux ferit ense ducem;
seu quia victa suis umeris haec arma ferebant,
  hinc Feretri dicta est ara superba Iovis

1–4. Now I shall begin to reveal the explanation of Juppiter Feretrius and the three sets of arms from three generals that he received. Great is the path I am climbing, but glory gives me strength; I do not like a garland gathered from an easy slope.

5–16. You baptize the example of the first of these victories, Romulus, and come enriched with your trophy from the enemy, at the time when Acron of Caenina makes for the gates and you victoriously send him sprawling with your spear on top of his overset horse. Acron, Hercules' son, a leader from Caenina's citadal, was once, Rome, an object to make your territory shudder. He ventured to hope for spoils from Quirinus' shoulders, but provided them himself, and drenched with his own blood. Romulus sees him brandishing his shafts in front of the hollow towers and anticipates him by a vow at once fulfilled:

'Juppiter, this is the victim that shall fall to you today, Acron.'
He ceased his vow, and the other falls, a spoil for Juppiter.

17–22. The City's and Virtue's father used thus to conquer, he who endured the camp's chill after his frugal home. He was a rider expert with reins, and expert too with the plough, and his helmet was of wolf hide, not decked with a hairy crest, his shield painted, not glittering with a layer of gold and bronze; slaughtered oxen provided his pliant belt.

23–30. Cossus comes next because of killing Tolumnius of Veii, when it took effort to be able to conquer Veii. Not yet was the sound of war heard beyond the Tiber, the furthest prey was Nomentum and the three-*iugera* allotments of captured Cora. Alas, ancient Veii, you too were then a great kingdom, and in your forum a golden throne was set; now within your walls the leisurely shepherd's horn sounds, and among your bones they harvest the fields.

31–8. As it chanced the Veientine leader took his stand on the gate tower, and parleyed confidently from his own city. And while the ram was striking the wall with its bronze horn, where the long shed covered the siege works going on, Cossus said:

'For a brave man it is better to clash in open field.'
Without delay, each takes his stand on the level. The gods helped the Latin's hands, Tolumnius' severed neck bathed in blood the Roman horses.

39–44. Claudius held off the enemy who had crossed from the Rhine, when he brought home the Belgic shield of their huge commander Virdomarus. He boasted his descent from Brennus himself, glorious for hurling javelins from a car he held on course. As he stained his striped breeches with blood, the hook-shaped collar fell from his cut throat.

45–8. Now there are three spoils stored in the temple; the explanation of 'Feretrius' is that, helped by a sure omen, leader smites (*ferit*) leader with his sword; or perhaps because they carried (*ferebant*) these vanquished spoils on their own shoulders, the proud altar is called that of Juppiter Feretrius.

As the only one of the aetiological poems dealing with feats of arms, the poem gets a special preface in which the poet emphasises the difficulty of his task. Throughout indeed his interventions are more frequent than in the other poems. He apostrophises Romulus with a strained phrase stressing the novelty of his achievement, he apostrophises Rome and, in unforgettable lines, the ruins of Veii; here and in the section on Romulus' armour he selects picturesque details to emphasise the contrast of past and present, and in the section on Virdomarus to highlight the exotic and strange; shunning the description of fighting, he gives a curt prayer to Romulus, a curt *sententia* to Cossus, and floods the three scenes with the blood of the defeated generals. At the end he brings the altar again before our eyes, as if we were the *hospes* of the first poem, and adds his explanation. Throughout, he is exerting himself to give a modern aspect to this most difficult of his subjects. One modern aspect he had however to shun: the *spolia opima* were won in 29 B.C. by M. Licinius Crassus; but no fourth set of spoils appeared in the temple of Juppiter Feretrius, because the *princeps* changed the rules and declared Crassus not eligible. The event illuminates the difficulties of a poet intent on being both Roman and contemporary. The best that Propertius can do is reiterate that there were three sets of spoils, 'three sets of arms from three generals', 'three spoils stored in the temple', and leave his reader to make what he can of it. Such poetry has no place for the bland scepticism of Livy who in one of his well-known 'refusals to go in for historical research' indicated that he had not bothered to go into the temple of Juppiter Feretrius and read the refurbished inscription on Cossus' breastplate which the *princeps* had assured him was there.

A comparison with the *Fasti* is again instructive. Like Propertius, Ovid in general shunned accounts of feats of arms; though the calendar presented him with several dates commemorating Roman victories and defeats, his report of them is usually restricted to a few couplets. But one exploit, the heroic self-sacrifice of the Fabian ancestors of his patron Paullus Fabius Maximus, he told at length and his telling shows what we miss in Propertius (*Fasti* 2.205 ff.):

> *Vt celeri passu Cremeram tetigere rapacem*   205
>   *(turbidus hibernis ille fluebat aquis),*
> *castra loco ponunt; destrictis ensibus ipsi*
>   *Tyrrhenum valido Marte per agmen eunt,*
> *non aliter quam cum Libyca de gente leones*
>   *invadunt sparsos lata per arva greges.*   210
> *diffugiunt hostes inhonestaque vulnera tergo*
>   *accipiunt; Tusco sanguine terra rubet.*
> *sic iterum, sic saepe cadunt; ubi vincere aperte*
>   *non datur, insidias armaque tecta parant.*
>
> *Campus erat, campi claudebant ultima colles*   215
>   *silvaque montanas occulere apta feras.*
> *in medio paucos armentaque rara relinquunt,*
>   *cetera virgultis abdita turba latet.*
> *ecce velut torrens undis pluvialibus auctus*
>   *aut nive, quae zephyro victa tepente fluit,*   220
> *per sata perque vias fertur, neque ut ante solebat*
>   *riparum clausas margine finit aquas,*
> *sic Fabii vallem latis discursibus implent,*
>   *quodque vident sternunt, nec metus alter inest.*
>
> *Quo ruitis, generosa domus? male creditis hosti.*   225
>   *simplex nobilitas, perfida tela cave.*
> *fraude perit virtus; in apertos undique campos*
>   *prosiliunt hostes et latus omne tenent.*
> *quid faciant pauci contra tot milia fortes?*
>   *quidve quod in misero tempore restet adest?*   230
> *sicut aper longe silvis Laurentibus actus*
>   *fulmineo celeres dissipat ore canes,*
> *mox tamen ipse perit, sic non moriuntur inulti*
>   *vulneraque alterna dantque feruntque manu.*

una dies Fabios ad bellum miserat omnes, 235
  ad bellum missos perdidit una dies.

Vt tamen Herculeae superessent semina gentis,
  credibile est ipsos consuluisse deos.
nam puer impubes et adhuc non utilis armis
  unus de Fabia gente relictus erat, 240
scilicet ut posses olim tu, Maxime, nasci
  cui res cunctando restituenda foret.

When their swift march has brought them to the raging Cremera (its flow was turbid with rain), they encamp; drawing their swords they make their way unsupported through the Etruscan line with sturdy fighting, just like lions of the Libyan breed rushing on flocks dispersed over broad fields. The enemy scatter, dishonourably wounded in the back; the earth is red with Tuscan blood. So they fall a second time, so often; when they fail to conquer openly, they prepare an ambush and covert arms.

There was a plain, its limits enclosed by hills and by a wood well able to conceal mountain beasts. In its centre they leave a few men and herds here and there, while the rest of the force lies hidden in the thickets. See! like a torrent swelling with rain or with snow melted by a warm West wind, spreading over fields and roads, no longer, as it used, firmly enclosing its waters within its banks, the Fabii fill the whole valley, ranging far and wide, and what they see they lay low, and feel no second fear.

Where are you rushing, highborn race? You do ill to trust the foe. Frank nobility, beware of treacherous weapons. Fraud brings down valour; everywhere the enemy dash out on to the open plain and occupy every flank. What can a few brave men do against all those thousands? What resource have they in their wretched straits? Like a boar after a long chase in the Laurentine woods, who scatters the swift hounds with the lightning of his tusks, yet at last perishes himself, they do not die unavenged, and give and take wounds alternately. One day had sent all the Fabii to war, one day destroyed all those sent forth.

Yet we can believe the gods took thought for the survival of the seed of Hercules' race. For a beardless boy, not yet fit for arms, was left, the only member of the Fabian family, doubtless so that in time to come you, Maximus, could be born to your task of saving the state by delay.

The first thing one can note is that Ovid has not so relentlessly

tried to accommodate this glorious defeat to the restrictions
of the elegiac mode; three similes and a description show that he
is not shrinking from epic techniques, though all are more
economical than in their epic use. Moreover, he is discreet in his
use of the stylistic features of elegy: he reserves apostrophe, for
instance, for the moment of crisis, so that it is not a mere man-
nerism but suggests an imagining so vivid that he cannot restrain
himself *now* from intervening. The first line of his last couplet,
with its cunning address to Maximus, suggests a reference to the
present day and his own patron (and Ovid does so use it elsewhere in a personal poem); but here the pentameter at once
removes the hint of the contemporary: the Fabius for whose birth
the gods took thought was the great Cunctator of the war with
Hannibal and the Roman epic tradition. Yet though it does not
shun grandeur, the passage is unmistakably elegiac, not epic, in
the way it singles out a few details for expansion and ruthlessly
contracts elsewhere and in its overall economy. What it evidences
and what Propertius' poem lacks is a sustained imagining that
makes the narrative flow continuously; instead of the pictorial
flashes of Propertius' stories we have a concentration on selected
aspects of a whole. Ovid, we feel, has imagined more than he tells
us, whereas with Propertius, and not only here, one has the
impression that the vivid moments he presents us with were
precisely what he himself saw, single pictures, not a developing
action. And it is perhaps in this characteristic of Propertius'
imagination, eminently pictorial but oddly disconnected (see
further below, pp. 164 ff.), that we should look for the reason why
the writing of the Roman *Aetia* was reserved for Ovid; the very
qualities that gave life and colour to the personal poems were a
downright impediment to the creation of a larger structure.

Whatever the date of its composition, the faults and virtues of the
Actium poem are much the same as those of the poems we have
been considering, and Propertius has taken care to accommodate
it to the aetiological genre. Its manner is strenuously Callimachean (below, p. 160), its professed theme is topographical,
the temple of the Palatine Apollo, which Propertius implies

(falsely) was the reward for Apollo's support at Actium, its structure suggests the idea of a rite, where the poet is first priest and then reporter of a celebration in Apollo's honour. It is not impossible that much of the poem does belong to the unfinished *Aetia* and that, as its style rather indicates, it is nearer in time to Book III than the group of poems that we shall come to next. In its concluding section however (from line 75), we have not only a mention (77) of an event of 16 B.C., Augustus' victory over the Sygambri, but an allusion to the adoption in 17 B.C. of Gaius and Lucius Caesar (82). The scene also has been transformed: the priestly poet of the opening lines is now one of a poetic company at dinner, with different poets hymning different achievements of the *régime*, the victory over the Sygambri, the exploits in Ethiopia (22 B.C.), the recovery of Crassus' standards from Parthia (20 B.C.). Very possibly, this concluding section is an addition that brings the earlier poem on Actium up to date, celebrating among other things the recent widening of Augustus' family and his latest victory. Of the bulk of the poem we can say that its manner is consonant with that of the Propertius who in Book III conceived the Roman *Aetia* and that it shows knowledge of the *Aeneid* (of which, of course, Propertius had already been by some method aware when he wrote 2.34).

In describing what was depicted on the shield of Aeneas Virgil had sketched a series of scenes which, though possible pictorial subjects, were all instinct with vigorous movement: Augustus leading the Italians to war, the star of Caesar obscured by the flames flaring from his head, Agrippa *arduus agmen agens*, the tumult of the battle itself with the foaming sea, the hurtling fire-bolts, Cleopatra summoning her columns with an Egyptian rattle, the combat of the gods, Mars raging, Discordia on her way, Bellona following, Apollo drawing his bow, the eastern hordes turning in flight, the escape of Cleopatra and her reception by the mourning Nile, the triumph of Caesar and procession of the conquered nations.

Propertius by contrast aims at stillness, beginning with an epic-style *ecphrasis* of the locale of the battle, the deep quiet gulf with its wide expanse of water, on it an unmoving mass of pine (*stetit aequore moles pinea*). The mass is divided and the two parts of it distinguished by their destiny, one already forfeit to Quirinus, the deified Romulus, one where the flagship has its sails swollen by Jove's propitious signs, and distinguished also each by a characterising detail, heavy javelins in a woman's hand (Antonius has no part in this Actium), the images of the gods on Augustus' poop. The stillness is broken by one movement of which we see the result, not the process (25 f.):

> *Tandem aciem geminos Nereus lunarat in arcus,*
> *armorum et radiis picta tremebat aqua.*

At length the sea god had arched the line into a double crescent and the water was quivering, coloured by the flash of arms.

The movement has been replaced by renewed quiet, now decisively interrupted by the advent of Phoebus and the flash of the thunderbolt. Action is once more suspended as he addresses words of encouragement to Caesar and promises his personal support. The battle begins at line 55 with the volley of Apollo's arrows and is over by 58, the symbols of Cleopatra's regal power (*sceptra* Propertius calls the wrecks in an audacious equation) drifting scattered on the Ionian sea. Two sketched scenes underline the result, the dance of the sea gods round Augustus' ship, Cleopatra making for the Nile in a desperate skiff. The rite of which Propertius professed himself priest in the opening section is resumed as the terrible Apollo of Actium takes up again his role of *citharoedus* and the feasting poets sing of Augustus' subsequent achievements. There are probably few readers of Propertius who find 4.6 their favourite poem; its restraint and the disciplining of fancy necessary in a poet attempting to write of Actium after Virgil make it seem something of a cold *tour de force*, for all its incidental beauties. But it provokes a reluctant admiration for all that.

Several poems of this book raise the question whether by 16 B.C. Propertius' art was already being affected by that of the young Ovid, by then about twenty-eight years old and, he tells us, precocious in poetry. The relevant poems (3 and 5) share the characteristic of either reporting or purporting to be the words of a woman, which we also find in this book in the Tarpeia poem, the monologue of the dead Cynthia and the speech of the dead Cornelia (4, 7, 11). This is not here novel in Propertius: he had already given Cynthia's words in 1.3 and (repeated from the report of the slave Lygdamus) in the dramatic monologue 3.6. But these earlier instances are much less ambitious and extended than those of Book IV; the monologues of Dido had of course intervened meanwhile and given Roman poets a new target to aim at.

One of the poems relevant to Ovid is 5, where a speech, set in the framework of a curse poem, is put in the mouth of a bawd trying to persuade the poet's mistress to exploit her beauty for gain. The frame, the curse, seems to have an imagined occasion, after the bawd's death, with an opening prayer for an overgrown grave and for her torment by thirst and the fiends, and at the end a vivid description of her fatal illness and a renewed curse on her grave. (Some have denied she is dead, but the relevant lines 9–11 are probably vivid rather, the poet's fear of her power leading him to speak as if it still operated.) The hyperbolical description of her dangerous persuasiveness which follows the first lines leads to her speech, introduced by an imperfect tense. What sort of an imperfect is this? General—'She used to ply her trade by saying what follows'—so that the speech, like the lover's serenade reported by the door in 1.16, is offered rather as a typical specimen of her skill, and we need not ask how the poet got to know of it? Or is it a properly narrative tense—'She was plying . . .'? In the latter case Propertius would be attempting a more sophisticated structure, with a dramatic soliloquy enshrining the report of a dramatic moment. We find this in him elsewhere, in the deft and lively setting of 3.6, where the poet urges Lygdamus to tell him all over again what he has already told him, then himself joyfully rehearses the speech of Cynthia that Lygdamus had reported and finally sends Lygdamus back with his answer to her. Have we something of equal refinement here? Not according to the manuscripts, but some scholars have argued that we should produce it if we do not have it.

After the bawd's speech, the manuscripts present us with this (63 ff.):

His animum nostrae dum versat Acanthis amicae,
  per tenues ossa sunt numerata cutes.
sed cape torquatae, Venus o regina, columbae   65
  ob meritum ante tuos guttura secta focos.
vidi ego rugoso tussim concrescere collo,
  sputaque per dentis ire cruenta cavos,
atque animam in tegetes putrem exspirare paternas;
  horruit algenti pergula curva foco.

While Acanthis thus tried to turn my mistress's mind, bones were numbered through thin skins. But accept the cut throat of a collared dove, Venus, o queen, for your services, slaughtered at your hearth. I have seen (or 'I saw') the cough swell in her wrinkled neck, and bloody spittle flow between the gaps of her teeth, and her breathing out her rotting spirit on her old family bedding; the sagging lean-to shivered with the fire burning low.

In this passage the second line, 'Bones were numbered through thin skins', is in any case unmetrical nonsense. But should we in correcting it aim to produce 'My bones were counted through my thin skin' or 'Her bones were counted through her thin skin'? 'But accept . . .' suggests the former; in that case Propertius is saying that the effect of Acanthis' speeches on his mistress reduced him to skin and bone, the earlier imperfect should be taken to mean 'She used to ply her trade . . .', and there is no specific setting for the speech.

To secure a dramatic setting we have to resort to transposition as well as emendation: two suggestions are offered, one simpler, one more complicated. The simpler transposes the first two couplets:

But (accept the cut throat of a collared dove, Venus, o queen, for your services, slaughtered at your hearth) while Acanthis thus tried to turn my mistress's mind, I counted her bones through her thin skin. I saw . . .

But if we want a sudden dramatic moment, the words 'While Acanthis was thus speaking, I counted her bones' do not seem to provide it, unless we suppose that she suddenly shrank to skin and bones like Ayesha in *She*; hence the more complicated hypothesis that 64 and 70 should also be interchanged:

But (accept the cut throat of a collared dove, Venus, o queen, for your services, slaughtered at your hearth) while Acanthis thus tried to turn my mistress's mind, the sagging lean-to shivered with the fire burning low. I saw the cough swell in her wrinkled neck, and bloody spittle flow between the gaps of her teeth, and her breathing out her rotting spirit on her old family bedding; I counted her bones through her thin skin.

This Professor Goold vigorously paraphrases as ' "in the midst of her speech"—what happened? . . . the fire went out, and Acanthis was attacked by a fatal fit of coughing'.

This is admirable sense, and it is worth stressing once more that though its dealings with the manuscripts are violent, they are not, in a tradition like that of Propertius, unjustifiably so. Yet the setting thus triumphantly achieved for Acanthis' speech is not altogether a likely one, and the reconstruction raises as many problems as it tries to deal with. In particular, it prompts questions of probability from which the manuscript order of the lines can claim exemption. The locale of the interview now becomes Acanthis' 'sagging lean-to', and this we do not expect; elsewhere in literature the tempting bawd is generally (and convincingly) a visitor to the lady. But even if we suppose the poet's mistress is calling in this unsavoury quarter, why is the poet there too? And where is he? In the room? Peeping through the door? Spying or complaisant? How does he see what he says he sees? Once the speech has a specific locale and such a surprising one, once it is set at a particular moment, we are entitled to demand more information than we are here given.

As we saw, Propertius' other practice could be invoked to support either of the hypotheses that the speech is a general specimen of Acanthis' eloquence (as in 1.16) or that it is a reported monologue in a setting (as in 3.6). What commends the latter interpretation is the Ovidian parallel in *Amores* 1.8; to quote Professor Goold again:

'in the midst of her speech'—what happened? Clearly, something which brought it to an abrupt end, just as Dipsas' speech in Ovid was brought to an abrupt end when he betrayed his presence.

But this Ovidian parallel may be delusive, and Ovid's economy here as elsewhere more rigorously governed by the strict laws of comedy. So it is, for example, precisely in the lover's serenade of which Propertius makes the door give a specimen in 1.16, while Ovid's address to the janitor (*Amores* 1.6), moving through the topics of persuasion and threats, carefully marking the passage of time from late evening till dawn, belongs to a single imagined situation. The poem on the bawd is similarly strict. In Propertius' poem it is possible to debate whether the bawd is alive or dead; Ovid's first word removes any doubt, *Est quaedam . . . nomine Dipsas anus.* Propertius' introductory imperfect leaves the status of Acanthis' speech vague; Dipsas' speech is preceded by a stage direction (*Amores* 1.8.21 f.):

Chance made me a witness. This was her advice (I was concealed by the double doors).

It is in keeping with this rigour that a similar direction breaks off her speech (109):

She was still running on when my shadow betrayed me.

No such tightness of form demands an equivalent causal nexus in Propertius' poem.

It is perhaps possible to go further and say that if Acanthis' speech is broken off by an event, this spoils the (non-causal) nexus that Propertius has created. The bawd ends her insinuating plea with the invocation of personal experience (59 ff.):

> *Dum vernat sanguis, dum rugis integer annus,*
> *utere, ne quid cras libet ab ore dies.*
> *vidi ego odorati victura rosaria Paesti*
> *sub matutino cocta iacere Noto.*

While your blood is at its spring, your years untouched by wrinkles, use it, for fear tomorrow the day may take from your beauty. I have seen the rose gardens of scented Paestum, that looked likely to live, scorched and blighted by a morning south wind.

vidi ego are her words, *eidon gar* in Greek, the standard phrase attesting an example from one's own experience. Must not

Propertius' own *vidi ego* only six lines further on be equally emphatic and of the same kind? To be equally emphatic they need to head the account of Acanthis' sufferings, as they do in the manuscripts, not come in the middle of the description as in the reconstructed texts. To be of the same kind they need to be not the mere reporting of an historic event ('I saw'), but the attestation of something significant ('I have seen'); and the only thing important enough for them to attest occurs in the preceding couplet, Venus' care for the poet, the service, the *meritum*, that earns his sacrifice. He has a guarantee of it: he has seen Acanthis afflicted. The death of the roses of Paestum supports one argument, the death of Acanthis supports a better and more powerful one. The logic of the structure here is not a dramatic one; it is not Acanthis and the poet who are in dialogue, but the poet is in dialogue with himself, assuring himself that his experience outattests hers.

This means that the balance of the two poems is very different. In Ovid the main stress is on Dipsas' speech (twice as long as that of Acanthis), with its ingeniously varied commendations of modern morals. The framework keeps this lengthy rhetoric within the genre of love elegy and sketches a likely scene. The poet's reactions are unelaborate and straightforward and are themselves what the stage could show (in the end he curses Dipsas, and just refrains from laying hands on her). In Propertius the 'frame' is at least as important as the speech, first developing the picture of his terror at Acanthis' power and then expressing his subsequent triumph. The disparate motifs that he employs are finally directed not to 'giving a genre picture of a bawd' or 'developing the topics of amatory precepts' but to expressing the lover's reactions, internalised and sometimes muffled, to this particular threat to his peace. One detail may point the difference: Ovid cheerfully puts into Dipsas' mouth a slander on Penelope (she set up the contest with the bow to test her youthful suitors' powers; no moral exemplar she but a pattern of utility); for Propertius' lover, it is a most signal instance of Acanthis' frightening power that she could even constrain Penelope to pay no attention to rumours of Ulysses' return and to marry the sportive

Antinous. Here and elsewhere, the paradox Propertius highlights is in the mind of the lover, not in the words of the bawd, and it is in this way that the poem aims at a more complex and difficult unity than Ovid's.

The other 'Ovidian' poem is the letter of a lady to her husband, absent on military service in the East. Like two of the addressees in the later part of Book II (Demophoon in 22, Lynceus in 34) and the slanderer Panthus of 2.21, they are given Greek names, though in this case they probably had pastoral rather than mythological connotations for Propertius, Arethusa and Lycotas. Neither here nor in Book II is there the slightest attempt to sustain the fiction that these Greek-named characters are Greek, much less figures of myth or pastoral; the names, that is, are treated as concealing pseudonyms and may indeed be so, used for reasons not easy to fathom.[1]

In 3.12 Propertius had treated a similar subject *in propria persona*, reproaching Postumus for deserting his wife Galla but assuring him of her fidelity, surpassing that of Penelope. Here he speaks in the person of a Roman Penelope herself, assigning to her a tender and jealous constancy, showing her starting from one emotion to another, prompted not so much by new ideas as by new images. Indeed her thinking is throughout not only prompted by but carried on in images, and presenting them to Lycotas is her method of argument. To send a letter is for her to imagine together both the reading and the writing of it (3 f.):

> *Si qua tamen tibi lecturo pars oblita derit,*
> *haec erit e lacrimis facta litura meis.*

If however you start to read it and find something rubbed out, the erasure will be caused by my tears.

To grieve at her lucklessness in marriage is to imagine the ceremony all awry, the wedding torch lighted from an overturned pyre, the ribbon on her head set crooked as at a funeral. Others

---

[1] Demophoon may be the poet who, Ovid suggests, was so nicknamed because he gave his mistress the pseudonym Phyllis, another Etruscan apparently (*Ex Ponto* 4.16.20), while Lynceus (dappled like a lynx) has been more hazardously identified with the poet and friend of Virgil, L. Varius.

might curse a vague 'inventor' of war or of swords; Arethusa's curse is for someone who plucked a fencing post for the camp from a tree that did not deserve it and who turned bones into trumpets. His fate should not be vague torment in Hades; instead (21 f.)

> *dignior obliquo funem qui torqueat Ocno*
> *aeternusque tuam pascat, aselle, famem.*

he deserves more than slantwise Ocnus to twist a rope and for all time feed your hunger, ass.

'Slantwise' because she recalls pictures of the unlucky Ocnus sitting twisting his rope in hell with the ass eating it as he twists. Another familiar picture, Hippolyte as an Amazon, barebreasted and helmed, suggests the wish that Arethusa too could go to the wars with Lycotas, 'a loyal bit of your baggage'. When she envisages Lycotas' danger and exploits, it is all particular, the mail-clad horses, painted chariots, swarthy Indians, the turban snatched from the scented head of an Eastern chief, the hail of sling stones. If she speaks of herself sacrificing, she sees the flowers, the little shrines, the sacral branches, the crossroads, the Sabine herb crackling on ancient fire-altars, the priestly butchers with their aprons girt up for the job. There is probably no poem in which Propertius so brilliantly exploits the peculiar character-istics of his own imagination to create another and convincing character.

What is suppressed is the rhetorical logic of his own thinking. Arethusa moves from picture to picture and from feeling to feeling, not from argument to argument. How far this statement is true is once more a matter of dispute, and here too quite large-scale transposition has been resorted to so as to restore rather more coherence to the progress of her ideas. But when we have laboured our best the result is still not *very* coherent, and in this poem above all one can reasonably wonder whether the whole attempt is not misguided; as well attempt, perhaps, to impose order on a mountain stream as on the transparent flow of Arethusa's consciousness, easily turned aside by any pebble.

Few ancient poems escape entirely from the world of rhetoric and the skilfully varied redeployment of the expected topic; and a consequence is that, in contrast to the resourceful mastery that classical poetry shows in the delineation of the passions, we find in much of it a flattening in the depiction of character. All this common stock of argument and ingenuity tends to make everybody a bit too clever. The fault is often identified as Ovid's, notably in Dryden's beautiful characterisation of him (Preface to the '*Translations from Ovid's Epistles*'):

Yet, not to speak too partially in his behalf, I will confess that the copiousness of his wit was such that he often writ too pointedly for his subject, and made his persons speak more eloquently than the violence of their passion would admit: so that he is frequently witty out of season; leaving the imitation of Nature, and the cooler dictates of his judgment, for the false applause of Fancy.

But the trouble is seated much more deeply than in Ovid's inability to stop; he presents only an extreme case of antiquity's affirmation of the supremacy of the intellect. Often, of course, this affirmation produces the right result: Oedipus, Medea, or Dido, by repute and achievements, can be as intelligent in the deployment and analysis of their passions as one chooses. But the immense procession of relentlessly self-aware and persuasive heroes and heroines can tax the mind, and this intellectualism certainly imposed a limitation rarely overstepped. It is part of the singular charm of Arethusa that by denying her efficient use of the rhetoric of persuasion, by showing her concentrated on the effort to make Lycotas see what she sees, never mind inference or connexion, Propertius has produced one of the few portraits antiquity offers of a good and beautiful noodle, loving, tender, and not in the least clever or formidable.

When one is contemplating artistry of such subtlety and refinement it is perhaps pointless to ask whether once more it was the originality of another poet that set Propertius off. Had he heard some of the *Amores* or some of the *Heroides* and been again prompted to rivalry? Dryden assumed it, and may be reckoned to have a better nose for such things than most of us:

I remember not any of the Romans who have treated this subject, save only Propertius, and that but once, in his Epistle of *Arethusa to Lycotas*, which is written so near the style of Ovid that it seems to be but an imitation; and therefore ought not to defraud our poet of the glory of his invention.

The judgement is a delimited one, 'written so near the style of Ovid'. Dryden is certainly not speaking of the structural economy of the poem, in which he regarded Propertius as deficient:

they [Propertius and Tibullus] can drive to no certain point, but ramble from one subject to another, and conclude with somewhat which is not of a piece with their beginning . . . But our Poet has always the goal in his eye, which directs him in his race; some beautiful design . . .

What Dryden is perhaps pointing to is the extreme simplicity and naturalness of Arethusa's language, not a constant feature of Propertius' style even in this book, but from the beginning, so far as we can see, characteristic of Ovid. Candid, concrete and Latin, with none of the distortion and affectation that marks some even of the best of Roman poetry, that style is here triumphantly used to create not a firework display of the passions but, the rarest thing in Roman poetry, a character. To compare Arethusa with Dido is absurd; but she too lives and has her own nature, and to compare her with the Deianeira or Ismene of Sophocles is not quite such nonsense.

We have in 4.11 a somewhat similar *prosopopoeia*, where Propertius speaks in the character of a noble Roman matron, the dead Cornelia, one of the high patrician aristocracy, step-daughter of the *princeps*, wife of one of the last non-imperial censors, sister of the consul of 16 B.C., the year of her death. The poem is called the *regina elegiarum*, 'incomparably his best', and so on, not without recalcitrance from some, perhaps justified. Admittedly judgement here is hampered by a tradition more than usually defective: for sixty lines we lack even the flickering light shed by the Neapolitanus and have to reconstruct its text from two late copies. Moreover, some of those who most admire it by no means admire it in its present form, but shuffle its lines with more than

ordinary thoroughness and admire the result of that. Some re-
organisation is necessary, given that the poem as the manuscripts
present it contains accusatives with no verb to govern them and
imperatives directed to no particular address and similar beauties;
but where the limits of the utility of drastic remedies are in
question, criticism is not easy. But perhaps it is in any case
legitimate to ask whether we have been admiring the poem for the
right reasons anyway and whether it is not a cooler and more
detached creation than is sometimes suggested. The trouble here,
to be blunt, is that many male critics seem to be in love with
Cornelia; perhaps this is right, perhaps, that is, Propertius shared
the general *Schwärmerei*. But given his success in creating the
independent, fully realised character of Arethusa, one can ask at
any rate whether Cornelia was so inextricably tangled round his
heart strings as she is round those of some of his commentators.

The poem is ingenious in form, taking its starting point from
the address to the bereaved husband that we find on ancient tomb-
stones, a motif, that is, of genuine epigram, which is here the
introduction to Cornelia's speech in defence of her character
before the underworld judges. The claims she advances to a
favourable reception in the world of the dead are those that in real
life would have been made in a funeral speech by her husband or
children, so that we have a reversal of the expected. The form
enables the poet to give Cornelia's husband and children the
consoling assurance of her continuing care for them not in his own
person but through her words, a more graceful and tactful pro-
ceeding. But it also enables her partly to state and partly to convey
her own values, and there is an interesting lack of harmony
between what she says and what she conveys, that in art of this
maturity one cannot take to be imposed by the form the poet has
chosen.

Cornelia begins with the sombre consolatory commonplaces on
the irreversibility of death and the powerlessness of good repute
and high connexions to avert it; this is standard. A more vivid
and characteristic touch follows: she who speaks is now merely a
load for five fingers to scrabble for (see above, pp. 35 f.); so the
manuscripts say, and perhaps rightly, with a single letter variation

on the ordinary expression, 'a load five fingers can carry'. At this
point she turns to the streams of the underworld, assures them she
is harmless, and asks that Hades grant her the privilege of entry
(17 f.):

> *Immatura licet, tamen huc non noxia veni.*
> *det Pater hic umbrae mollia iura meae.*

Though I come before my time, I come not dangerous.[1] May the
Father here grant gentle privileges to my shade.

She then asserts her readiness to submit to judgement and urges a
holiday for the great sinners and for Cerberus himself as she
makes her defence.

The terms of her defence state the ideals of her class. First and
foremost she is of unassailably high birth on both sides (there is
a little special pleading here: her maternal ancestors, the Scribonii
Libones, were in fact nothing like as grand as the Cornelii
Scipiones; but it was of course through her mother Scribonia that
she was connected with the *princeps*, and that justified a little
inflation). Secondly, she can boast on her tombstone that she was
univira, the wife of one husband, and that husband himself one of
the highest nobility. Thirdly, her life has been blameless (47 f.):

> *Mi Natura dedit leges a sanguine ductas,*
> *nec possis melior iudicis esse metu*

Nature gave me laws derived from my blood and fear of a judge could
not make one better.[2]

---

[1] Most commentators seem content to interpret this as 'Though I come before
my time, I come not guilty', sometimes adding a note to the effect that Cornelia is
asserting that her early appearance is not due to her having been put to death for
horrid crimes. But even apart from the fact that conventionally it is the good who
die young, not the wicked, why should the denizens of the underworld hastily
suppose that this noble lady is a criminal, so hastily that her very first words have
to remove their error? Does she look like Phaedra or Sthenoboea? On the other
hand, at the sight of one of the *aôroi*, those who die before their time, dangerous
haunters in ancient superstition, even the underworld people might want re-
assurance that she was not proposing to exercise the sinister powers that status
conferred.

[2] We are told that the note of defiance is 'most improper in Cornelia's address
to the judge'. So it might be if it were not a member of the Roman aristocracy
speaking; but that was how they did speak. So Metellus Celer reproached Cicero

Her company will not disgrace the patrician paragons of Roman tradition, the chaste Claudia and the Vestal Aemilia. Fourthly, she is defended by the tears of her mother Scribonia, the laments of Rome and the sobs of Caesar himself (59 f.):

Ille sua nata dignam vixisse sororem
increpat, et lacrimas vidimus ire deo.

He reproaches the fates that a sister worthy of his own daughter has died and we have seen tears flow from the god's eyes.

Events made the detail infelicitous, but the disgrace of Julia was still far in the future. Fifthly, she has seen her brother praetor and consul, dying in his consulship. Sixthly, in spite of this early death, she has earned the privileges recently assigned by the *princeps* to the mother of three children.

These are her expressed claims. Better ones appear when in the final section she turns to console and advise her husband and children, urging him to conceal his grief from them, her sons to endure a stepmother if they have to or to comfort his widowhood if that is what he chooses, her daughter to have one husband as her mother has done.[1] For her children she wishes the years that she has not lived through, and children of their own, and so takes her farewell of them:

Quod mihi detractum est, vestros accedat ad annos; 95
prole mea Paullum sic iuvet esse senem.

---

with defending himself against the aggression of Celer's brother Nepos (*Fam.* 5.1.1 'If his own decent behaviour did not defend him, then either *the dignity of our family* or my support for you [plural, the *optimates*, not Cicero personally] and for the state should have helped him'). If dignity of the family could excuse personal insult and riot in the forum, it could certainly be invoked to repel a judge's injurious suspicion that one had refrained from sin for fear of punishment.

[1] It is hard to doubt that the last section of the poem is in confusion, which editors sort out very variously. The order of lines supposed here is 85–94, 67–8, 71–2, 95–6, 69–70, 97–8. Those editors who remove to this point the lines addressed to the daughter (67–8, 71–2) put them after 96, confining the wish for long life to the sons. But it is then hard to find a place for 'support the race', which must be addressed to the children; and the rest of that couplet ('with so many of my own to magnify my deeds') seems to be underlined by 'I have never put on mourning' and to belong with it.

et serie fulcite genus; mihi cumba volenti 69
　solvitur aucturis tot mea facta meis. 70
et bene habet: numquam mater lugubria sumpsi;
　venit in exsequias tota caterva meas.

May the time taken from me be added to your years; given children of
mine may Paullus be glad then to be an old man. And support the race
by continuance; the skiff casts off with my good will with so many of
my own to magnify my deeds. And it is well: as a mother I have never
put on mourning; the whole throng has come to my funeral.

This consolatory section, imaginative, affectionate and rational,
is her real claim to a sympathetic reception among the shades, the
justification of her hope for a place in the heavens beside her
honoured ancestors. The moral content of the aristocratic ideal
here finds an expression beyond its own powers. Yet not all of
Cornelia's words move on this high level, and in one's thinking
about the poem and one's estimate of what Propertius achieves in
it it is wrong to underplay the arrogant Roman pride of race and
claim to privilege to which the Umbrian and municipal poet,
passionate, intelligent and Italian, also gives a voice unmistakably
its own.

There came to him the soul of hapless Patroclus, like himself in all,
size and handsome countenance and voice, and wearing the same
clothes. It stood at his head and said: 'Do you sleep and have no
memory of me, Achilles? You neglect me dead, though not alive. Bury
me so that at once I can pass the gates of Hades . . . And I bid you do
this too, if you will: do not put my bones apart from yours, Achilles,
but with them, just as we were brought up together in your halls, when
Menoetius brought me, a little boy, from Opus to you to escape the
manslaughter I had done on the day I killed the son of Amphidamas, all
unwitting, not meaning to, in anger over the knucklebones; then the
knightly Peleus welcomed me in his home and brought me up carefully and called me your squire; even so let a single jar conceal our
bones, golden, two-handled, the one your mother gave you.'
　Swiftfoot Achilles said in reply: 'Why have you come here, dear
head, and why bid me do all this . . .?'
　So he spoke and stretched out his arms, with no success; the soul
departed underground like smoke, squeaking as it went. Achilles was

astounded and jumped up, clapping his hands, and cried: 'Ah truly there is then in Hades' halls a soul, an image, but no living spirit in it. For this night the soul of hapless Patroclus stood over me weeping and lamenting and bade me do this and that, and was wonderfully like himself.'

This is the scene, rich for post-Homeric feeling with the erotic associations that made the joint grave of Achilles, Patroclus and the young Antilochus a pilgrimage centre for the romantic and sentimental, on which Propertius has founded the first of the two great Cynthia poems of this book, in which the ghost of the dead Cynthia reproaches the poet with his neglect of her memory and re-establishes her dominion over him. Editors oddly debate whether or not the ghost of Cynthia ever did disturb Propertius' sleeps, but the question is irrelevant; if she did, she certainly did not address him in the accents of Patroclus, and the genesis and justification of the poem are to be sought not in 'experience' but in the heightening of the contemporary and everyday that is gained from the exploitation of the high tragic and pathetic heroism of epic. This was something that had fascinated Propertius from the beginning when in 1.11 he appropriated the words of Andromache as his own (above, p. 56 n.1); but here it is given something better than the allusiveness that could exploit Homer for a load of associative emotion. This is Homer not merely recollected but transposed and modernised, to a world where characters of equal authenticity, however remote from the values, the strengths, the limitations of the heroic world, speak in the accents of their great predecessors. It is an acknowledgement that the imagination has power to reach over centuries, that the picture it presents remains valid for persons and in societies utterly different from those the original poet could envisage; far more than any blunt statement we have in other books and other poets, it displays the power of poetry to confer immortality, and not by shunning detail and the contingent. The society Cynthia inhabits is more complex, her words more full of particularity than those of Patroclus; but Patroclus remains an exemplar for her.

The differences between the two societies are stressed and illuminated by detail. What unites Cynthia and Propertius is not noble hospitality and antique purification for homicide, but secret meetings in the ever-wakeful Subura, her exploits in climbing down a rope to join him, their assignations at the crossroads. The details of the correct funeral he has denied her are all Roman and vivid. The society of slaves, the *meretrix* who has replaced her and who torments those loyal to her memory, fettering one old woman to a filthy log, tying up another girl by the hair and beating her, belong to the Roman world of sordid and brutal actuality that by and large the poets prefer to neglect. We could not be more remote from the society of the heroic age, more firmly located in the *verismo* of the mime.

This is not the only difference. Though the society is more ordinary, its aspirations are more romantic. Patroclus asks only for entry to the underworld and for common burial with Achilles. Cynthia is in the Elysium reserved for the faithful heroines, sped there in a garlanded yacht, to fields of gentle breezes and roses, with music on all sides: there with Andromeda and Hypermestra she confirms the love she felt in life by tears shed in death, loyally concealing her lover's treachery. The grave she asks for is a model of the picturesque, such as painting and poetry both commended, her presence and her request in a rational and philosophic age need explanation, the mingling of her bones with those of Propertius (not requested but prophesied) will not be a recognition of honour and friendship but is a complicated assertion of her continuing power (above, p. 31):

> Pone hederam tumulo, mihi quae praegnante corymbo
>   mollia contortis alliget ossa comis,   80
> ramosis Anio qua pomifer incubat arvis,
>   et numquam Herculeo numine pallet ebur.
> hic carmen media dignum me scribe columna,
>   sed breve, quod currens vector ab urbe legat:
> HIC TIBVRTINA IACET AVREA CYNTHIA TERRA;   85
> ACCESSIT RIPAE LAVS, ANIENE, TVAE.
>
> Nec tu sperne piis venientia somnia portis;
>   cum pia venerunt somnia, pondus habent.
> nocte vagae ferimur, nox clausas liberat umbras,
>   errat et abiecta Cerberus ipse sera.   90

luce iubent leges Lethaea ad stagna reverti;
nos vehimur, vectum nauta recenset onus.
nunc te possideant aliae; mox sola tenebo;
mecum eris, et mixtis ossibus ossa teram.

Plant ivy on my grave to entwine as its cluster swells my delicate bones
with its interlaced foliage, where the apple-bearing Anio rests in the
lowlying fields full of branches, and Hercules' power keeps ivory always
white. Here inscribe on a central column a poem worthy of me, but
brief, for the traveller hastening from the city to read:
> 'Here golden Cynthia lies in Tibur's soil; your bank has now
> more glory, Anio.'

And do not you contemn dreams that come through the righteous
gates; when righteous dreams come, they matter. By night we range as
we will, night frees the imprisoned shades, the door bolt lies on the
ground and Cerberus himself goes wandering. At dawn the laws bid us
return to Lethe's pools; we cross, and the ferryman counts his cargo.
For now let others have temporary ownership of you; soon I alone
shall hold you; you will be with me, and mingling my bones with yours
I shall press them hard.

Epic, tragedy, the mime, the epigram have all been turned to
account, the sentimental languors of Hellenistic eroticism, the
Romans' deep-lying terror at the dangerous realm of the dead,
their hardheaded appreciation of the actualities of the world; we
have come a long way since it made sense to do what we did at
the beginning, and analyse a poem of Propertius in terms of its
relation to the elegancies of Meleager.

Propertius followed this poem with one of great comic inventiveness, and one that is also closely related to it. One element in
his wit had long been the inversion of the expected roles of male
and female. That could be pushed further: if in 4.7 there is some
restraint in giving Cynthia the role of Patroclus and in thus
reserving to himself, if only by implication, that of Achilles, there
is none in 4.8, where Cynthia appears as the vengeful Odysseus,
Propertius as a Penelope less constant than her mythical pro-
genetrix. Probably few insights into Propertius in recent years
have been as useful as Mr. S. Evans' observation that the long
recognised relation between 4.7 and Book XXIII of the *Iliad* has

a parallel in the relation between 4.8 and the main plot of the *Odyssey*, a relation that declares itself not from the first line of the poem as in 4.7 but in the coincidence in numerous vivid details.[1] Propertius was, after all, one of the most self-conscious of poets, and in the ancient world that means among other things a poet aware of other people's thinking about poetry. From Aristotle to Longinus ancient criticism concurred in seeing in the *Iliad* the great poem of *pathos*, of the tragic emotions, in the *Odyssey* the great poem of *ethos* (manners), of moral character in a social context. Longinus expresses it most eloquently, but here as elsewhere his thought is not quite unprompted by the standard opinion of the cultivated (9.13–15):

Homer in the *Odyssey* may be compared to the setting sun: the size remains without the force. He no longer sustains the tension as it was in the tale of Troy, nor that consistent level of elevation which never admitted any falling off. The outpouring of passions crowding one on another has gone; so has the versatility, the realism, the abundance of imagery taken from the life . . . I want you to understand that the decline of emotional power in great writers and poets turns to a capacity for depicting manners. The realistic description of Odysseus' household forms a kind of comedy of manners.

Between 4.7 and 4.8 Propertius exhibits a similar relation, and the tragic heightening that his relation with Cynthia sustained in 4.7 is in 4.8 displaced when the same relation is displayed on the level of a 'kind of comedy of manners'.

The poem starts with a solemn preface, professing a pregnant immediacy that some have innocently supposed might be fact (but poems of this elaboration are not scribbled overnight):

> *Disce quid Esquilias hac nocte fugarit aquosas,*
> *cum vicina novis turba cucurrit agris*

Learn what this night caused a riot among the fountains of the Esquiline, when the crowd of neighbours rushed about in the new-made fields.

It continues with something not only solemn but, in a book containing aetiological poems, deliberately misleading:[2]

---

[1] *Greece and Rome* 18, 1971, 51 ff. So also H. Currie, *Latomus* 32, 1973, 616 ff.
[2] Some put after this first couplet lines 19f. 'when a disgraceful brawl resounded

Lanuvium annosi vetus est tutela draconis,
  hic ubi tam rarae non perit hora morae,
qua sacer abripitur caeco descensus hiatu,   5
  qua penetrat virgo (tale iter omne cave),
ieiuni serpentis honos cum pabula poscit
  annua et ex ima sibila torquet humo.
talia demissae pallent ad sacra puellae,
  cum temere anguino creditur ore manus.   10
ille sibi admotas a virgine corripit escas;
  virginis in palmis ipsa canistra tremunt.
si fuerint castae, redeunt in colla parentum,
  clamantque agricolae 'Fertilis annus erit'.

Lanuvium is the ancient ward-place of a long-lived serpent, here where
time spent on so precious a delay is not wasted, where the holy descent
falls sheer in a dark gulf, where a maiden makes her way (beware of
any such path), when the hungry revered serpent[1] demands his annual
feed and writhes his hisses from the depths of the ground. Such are the
rites to which girls are lowered, all pale, when their hands are rashly
entrusted in the snaky mouth. He gobbles the food a maiden proffers;
in the maiden's hands the very baskets tremble. If they are chaste, they
return to their parents' embrace, and the farmers cry 'The year will be
fruitful'.

The reader has already met sacred places and explanatory rites
in poems 2, 4 and 6 of this book and has been promised something
similar in poem 1. Whatever he next expects after this elaborate
and high-sounding preface, it is not what he gets, an account of
Cynthia's misconduct at this festival in the company of a 'depi-
lated wastrel', destined to a low gladiatorial career 'when the

---

in a secret tavern, if without me yet not without stain to my repute'. But wherever
this belongs (not where the manuscripts give it) it does not belong here, where it
ruins the mock mystery of the opening section.

[1] 'The honour of the hungry serpent' in a grandiose locution over-frequent in
Propertius, often with less justification than here (so Passerat; one might
especially compare Sophocles' *theôn hagnon sebas* in *Oed. Tyr.* 830). Modern
editors tend to punctuate *qua penetrat (virgo, . . . cave!)* and take *ieiuni serpentis
honos* as the subject of *penetrat*. But when an ancient reader met *qua penetrat virgo*
(which after all she does), how was he meant to realise that these words were in
no syntactical relation to each other and that he must wait for another and more
puzzling subject of *penetrat*? Editors proudly record that the bracket before *virgo*
is Scaliger's; they do not record that he read *penetral*.

beard he is ashamed of finally vanquishes his shaven cheeks'. The misconduct is perhaps heightened even by blasphemy: why else the detailed description of Cynthia's triumph as she drove her own chariot along the Appian way, in the posture of the goddess of the festival as we see her depicted on coins of Lanuvium?[1] Penelope could complain of much in Odysseus' behaviour, but not this much. And Propertius, moved by insult and outrage, was less long-suffering than she; to console himself, he invited in two girls. With economy and verve, he describes the party, the bad omens that attended it, the return of a Cynthia intent on vengeance, her rout of the girls, subjection of himself, and purification of the house. The elements are those of the *Odyssey*, but the motives for manners are different these days: the ritual purification that cleared Odysseus' palace of the pollution of the suitors' death has become a comic act of superstition to clear away all taint of the alien girls. Once more, as we have seen so often before, a comic inversion undercuts a statement of solemn import: if 4.7 says that the accents of passion have resonance over the centuries, 4.8 admits it but insinuates the question whether, if we could give more context to the high passions and actions of antiquity, they would look so very high. Propertius had evaded the question in the opening poem of Book III (3.1.23 ff.):

> *Omnia post obitum fingit maiora vetustas;*
> *maius ab exsequiis nomen in ora venit.*
> *nam . . .*
> *exiguo sermone fores nunc, Ilion, et tu*
> *Troia bis Oetaei numine capta dei.*
> *nec non ille tui casus memorator Homerus*
> *posteritate suum crescere sensit opus.*
> *meque inter seros laudabit Roma nepotes;*
> *illum post cineres auguror ipse diem.*

Antiquity shapes everything more impressive after death; one's name comes grandly into men's mouths when the funeral is over. Otherwise . . . you would be little talked of, Ilion, and you, Troy twice captured by the god who died on Oeta. Yes, and he who told your fate, Homer, felt his work grow greater with the generations. Me too Rome will

---

[1] K. Latte, *Römische Religionsgeschichte*, Munich, 1960, Pl. 10b.

praise in the time of our distant descendants; after I am ash I divine that day will come.

Retrieving the false step that he had made into grandiosity with his ambition after the great *Aetia,* he demonstrated in 4.7 and 4.8 that there was more than one valid way of interpreting the experience of antiquity.

CHAPTER FIVE

Retrospect

THE 'style' of Propertius' poetry is, I have tried to show, no such thing. More than most of the Roman poets he is a chamaeleon and an experimenter, and what can truly be said of one book or even of one poem cannot be said of another. The manner of Tibullus, the manner of Horace, the manner no doubt of Gallus all affect him, and there are moments when the influence of other poets produces an almost parodic effect. One instance of this looks to be found in 1.20 (above, pp. 37 ff.). It is no less apparent in Book III, where the imagistic technique that Propertius derived from Callimachus modified by Horace sometimes results in a pyrotechnic display that may seem too much of a good thing. The effect is marked in the rapid substitution of image for image in the first poem of the book (above, p. 76). It is equally present towards the end, in 3.24 (for the purpose it there serves, see above, p. 92):

> *Falsa est ista tuae, mulier, fiducia formae,*
> *olim oculis nimium facta superba meis.*
> *noster amor talis tribuit tibi, Cynthia, laudes;*
> *versibus insignem te pudet esse meis.*
> *mixtam te varia laudavi saepe figura,*   5
> *ut quod non esses esse putaret amor;*
> *et color est totiens roseo collatus Eoo,*
> *cum tibi quaesitus candor in ore foret.*
>
> *Quod mihi non patrii poterant avertere amici,*
> *eluere aut vasto Thessala saga mari,*   10
> *hoc ego non ferro, non igne coactus, et ipsa*
> *naufragus Aegaea (vera fatebor) aqua.*
>
> *Correptus saevo Veneris torrebar aeno;*
> *vinctus eram versas in mea terga manus.*
> *ecce coronatae portum tetigere carinae,*   15
> *traiectae Syrtes, ancora iacta mihi est.*

nunc demum vasto fessi resipiscimus aestu,
vulneraque ad sanum nunc coiere mea.
Mens Bona, si qua dea es, tua me in sacraria dono.
exciderant surdo tot mea vota Iovi.   20

1–8. You are wrong, woman, to be confident in your beauty, you whom my eyes once made all too tyrannical. It was my love conferred such merit on you, Cynthia; I am ashamed my lines made you glorious. I praised you as made up of varied beauties so that love supposed you what you were not; and often I compared your complexion to the rosy dawn, when the brilliant whiteness on your face was imported.

9–12. What my father's friends could not remove from me, nor the Thessalian witch wash out with the vast sea, this I have got rid of, not constrained by surgery or cautery, shipwrecked, I shall confess, on an Aegean sea (of love).

13–20. I had caught fire and was being roasted in Venus' cruel bronze; I had had my hands bound behind my back. See! my ships are garlanded and have come to port; the sandbanks are crossed, my anchor cast. Now at last, weary from the vast surge, I recover sense, and now my wounds have scabbed over. Good Sense, if you are a goddess, I dedicate myself in your shrine; Jove was deaf and paid no heed to all my prayers.

Even in one detail of technique the poem approaches pastiche of Horace: when Propertius says

and often I compared your complexion to the rosy dawn, when the brilliant whiteness on your face was imported,

he uses, and perhaps uses here only, a trick that Horace uses constantly. He singles out for vividness two quite different details the conjunction of which produces an irrationality that disappears if one substitutes general terms for the particular ones, says here, for instance, 'I gave extravagant praise to your complexion, when it was all due to make-up'. The distribution between two clauses of the pink and white of Cynthia's complexion corresponds to the distribution of the gifts in Horace, *Odes* 4.8.1 ff.:

I should like to give plate, bronze statues and tripods to my friends, and paintings or marble statues to you.

In Horace this sort of thing is so common that most of his editors do not even bother to comment on it, in Propertius so rare that commentators here have been excessively puzzled and have advanced unpersuasive interpretations of *candor*, pretending, for instance, that 'whiteness' means 'pinkness'. In fact, the uncharacteristic turn shows him alert to exploit an Horatian elegancy.

Something similar is true of the clashing series of images that concludes the poem. They resemble the images of Horace both in their allusiveness (the Aegean is the sea of love because *Aegaea* is an epithet of Venus, and 'Venus' cruel bronze' suggests the image of Phalaris' bull that in 2.25.12 Propertius uses explicitly to define love's sufferings, above, p. 66) and in the way each flashes on our gaze and is then instantly replaced by another. If we look for parallels to this in Latin poetry, it is to the *Odes* that we must turn, to the end, for instance, of 2.3, where the man destined to death is a blood-sacrifice to the pitiless god of the underworld, a beast in the herd of shades, a name written on a lot, a passenger in Charon's boat bound for perpetual exile.

A similar parade of metaphor opens a later poem that overtly alludes both to Callimachus and to the first ode of Horace's third book. Callimachus' hymn to Apollo had represented poet and chorus as waiting for the advent of the god and had urged silence for the hymn (1 ff.):

How the shoot of Apollo's bay has quivered, how the whole hall! Away, away, any sinner. Surely Phoebus is knocking the door with his lovely foot. Do you not see? The Delian palm has suddenly nodded sweetly, and the swan in the air is singing a fine song. Open of yourselves, you fastenings of the doors, of yourselves, you keys; for the god is no longer far off. You lads, prepare for dance and song . . . Be silent all as you listen to Apollo's song. Even the sea falls silent when bards hymn either lyre or arrows, the weapons of Lycorean Phoebus.

Horace too had urged silence on the crowd as he, the priest of the Muses, began his new and ambitious song at the opening of *Odes III*. Propertius takes up a similar stance to hymn Actium (4.6.1 ff.):

Sacra facit vates; sint ora faventia sacris
et cadat ante meos icta iuvenca focos.
cera Philiteis certet Romana corymbis,
et Cyrenaeas urna ministret aquas.
costum molle date et blandi mihi turis honores,   5
terque focum circa laneus orbis eat.
spargite me lymphis, carmenque recentibus aris
tibia Mygdoniis libet eburna cadis.
ite procul fraudes, alio sint aere noxae.
pura novum vati laurea mollit iter.   10

The poet-priest is celebrating rites; let silence attend them and a heifer
fall at a blow before my fire. Let a Roman writing tablet vie with
Philetas' ivy berries and the urn supply Cyrenaean [i.e. Callimachean]
water. Give me luxurious putchuk, offerings of persuasive incense, and
let the ring of wool go three times round the fire. Sprinkle me with
sacral water and let the ivory flute make a libation of song[1] from
Phrygian jars on fresh-cut altars. Away with you, fraud; crime, dwell
under another sky. His unblemished bay makes the priest's new path
soft.

Once more the riot of imagery accompanies the adoption of an
imposing posture. It is perhaps unfortunate for Propertius'
reputation that this style, not all that frequent in him, is often
treated as characteristic; this sort of Propertius is, notably, the
one most nearly presented to amateurs of Roman poetry in the
imitations of Pound, in which even Propertius' ironies tend to
assume an unduly emphatic tone. Yet Propertius' successes in this
style, though real, are few, many fewer than those of his two
exemplars. A principal reason for this is that, not always but often,
the manner brings with it the suggestion of a public stance, a
public *persona*. Both the manner and the stance descend to Callimachus himself from the aristocratic assurance of Pindar: the poet
is priest or prophet, his words an oracle to be comprehended by
the initiated; an intense conviction of one's worth as a poet is
built in to such a style. Not, of course, that it excludes the high
irony of the utterly self-confident; but the irony is itself a posture,
a part of good manners. If the conviction of one's personal value

---

[1] The image is Pindar's, a poet no favourite of Propertius, but one who had
deep influence on Callimachus and Horace.

is less than total, the irony too departs, and a tumid self-aggrandisement is all that is left. For Propertius, supple, self-aware, self-questioning, the oracular pose was not one that came naturally, and except where he could, as in the opening poems of Book III, adapt it to his normal investigatory manner, he does not often look comfortable in it or use its language with the restrained mastery of Callimachus or Horace.

This sort of imagism is, to repeat, frequent in Book III and retained in a few, not most, poems of Book IV. Its failures and successes are those generally pointed to by those wishing to delineate a distinctively 'Propertian' style; and it is only the wilder excesses of this particular style that give any colour to those who characterise as 'Propertian' the yet more excessive idiosyncrasies of his manuscripts. To counter the impression these excesses foster it is worth looking at one poem of great elegance and simplicity of style, where plain words flexibly indicate a situation and a complex range of reactions to it; the poem, as 'Propertian' as any, is the antecedent in Book II to the more exquisite masterpiece of the letter of Arethusa, and is itself epistolary (cf. above, p. 52 n.1), its manner perhaps a surprise to those whose judgement of Propertius is guided by the more excitable accounts. Propertius is at home on his estate (*hic* of line 29) and writes to Cynthia who is proposing to leave Rome and stay in *villeggiatura* somewhere in the country (2.19):

> *Etsi me invito discedis, Cynthia, Roma,*
> *   laetor quod sine me devia rura coles.*
> *nullus erit castis iuvenis corruptor in agris,*
> *   qui te blanditiis non sinat esse probam;*
> *nulla neque ante tuas orietur rixa fenestras* 5
> *   nec tibi clamatae somnus amarus erit.*
> *sola eris et solos spectabis, Cynthia, montis*
> *   et pecus et finis pauperis agricolae.*
> *illic te nulli poterunt corrumpere ludi,*
> *   fanaque peccatis plurima causa tuis.* 10
> *illic assidue tauros spectabis arantis,*
> *   et vitem docta ponere falce comas;*
> *atque ibi rara feres inculto tura sacello,*

haedus ubi agrestis corruet ante focos;
protinus et nuda choreas imitabere sura,   15
omnia ab externo sint modo tuta viro.

Ipse ego venabor: iam nunc me sacra Dianae
suscipere et Veneris ponere vota iuvat.
incipiam captare feras et reddere pinu
cornua et audaces ipse monere canis—   20
non tamen ut vastos ausim temptare leones
aut celer agrestis comminus ire sues.
haec igitur mihi sit lepores audacia mollis
excipere aut structo figere avem calamo,
qua formosa suo Clitumnus flumina luco   25
integit, et niveos abluit unda boves.

Tu quotiens aliquid conabere, vita, memento
venturum paucis me tibi Luciferis.
hic me nec solae poterunt avertere silvae,
nec vaga muscosis flumina fusa iugis,   30
quin ego in assidua mussem tua nomina lingua,
absenti nemo ne nocuisse velit.

1–16. Even though I am sorry you are leaving Rome, Cynthia, I am glad that in our separation you will be living in the out-of-the-way countryside. There will be no lad in the chaste fields to seduce you and flatter you into misdeeds; no squabble will arise outside your windows, no shouts to make your sleep less sweet. You will be alone and will gaze at the lonely mountains, Cynthia, and the flock and the poor farmer's lands. There no games will be able to corrupt you, no temples, the multiple cause of your wrong-doing. There you will spend your time watching the bulls ploughing, and the vine lay aside its tresses under the skilled sickle; and there you will bring a fine scattering of incense to an unadorned little shrine, when the goat falls victim before the rustic fires; and you will go on to mimic dances, bare-legged, always providing there is no danger of an intruder.

17–26. I myself shall be hunting: even now my pleasure is to take up Diana's rites and lay aside Venus'. I shall set about snaring beasts and duly giving their horns to a pine-tree and myself scolding the eager hounds—not, however, that I should venture to assail huge lions or dash to encounter wild boars. So let this be my bravery, to lie in wait for soft hares and fix a bird with a jointed fowling-rod, where Clitumnus shades its lovely streams with the wood it mirrors[1] and the wave washes the snowy oxen clean.

27–32. As for you, whenever you try something on, my life, remember I shall come to you in a few days. Here neither the lonely woods nor the vagrant streams pouring down from mossy ridges will be able to distract me from continually murmuring your name, forbidding any to wish to damage the absent.[2]

'*Pulcherrima elegia*', says Enk, with approving notice also of its '*simplices et amoeni versus*'; and though, like all Propertian elegies, the poem can be and has been misinterpreted, it contains no real difficulty except the conceit of the last couplet, where Propertius' iteration of Cynthia's name is apparently itself the means by which the magisterial decree forbidding damage to the absent is conveyed. Admittedly, even Book II and indeed even Book I contain few poems quite so straightforward as this. The reason is the comparative rarity of epistolary poems in Propertius: the epistolary genre brings with it the concreteness and directness that we find here, just as it dictates the use of ordinary words to Arethusa in 4.3 (the *lacerna* or military cloak, the soldier's baggage, *sarcina*, the sacerdotal butcher, *popa*, the diminutive *asellus*), and as it dictates to Propertius himself in 1.11 the use of the colloquial *mage* for *potius*, of the diminutive *parvula*, and of the polite imperatival future *ignosces* (this last, with a fine tact, borrowed from an epistolary poem of Catullus, 68.31). In other words, Propertius' style alters not only with differences of stance that result from changes in his poetic attitude over time, but because of the demands of a genre that is exemplified at various

---

[1] 'with its own wood' should mean more than 'with the wood that grows on its banks', but it may not mean as much as I am here suggesting.

[2] It was a fine instinct that led some humanist scribe to substitute *ne nocuisse velit* for the *non nocuisse velit* of the tradition. The double negative *nemo ne* instead of *ne quis* is a colloquialism that suits the poem's epistolary style. The perfect infinitive with *velit* has a technical and legal flavour that it has taken a lawyer to point out: 'The—rather rare—form of decree *ne quis fecisse velit* . . . originates in ordinances by magistrates to ensure public order and decency; . . . it is very energetic; . . . it conveys a nasty and, essentially, indeterminate threat of unpleasant consequences in the event of transgression' (David Daube in Luitpold Wallach (ed.), *The Classical Tradition, Literary and Historical Studies in Honor of Harry Caplan*, Cornell University Press, 1966, p. 222).

periods of his career. In both respects 2.19 and the prelude to 4.6 are at extreme poles; the question where, between these two poles, any particular poem is to be located is not one that can be answered by over-hasty inductions about the distinctively 'Propertian'.

Far more constant than style is the nature of Propertius' imagination, more vividly pictorial than that of any other Augustan poet except Virgil, but active in a quite different way. What we find in Virgil is the power to present successive images as part of a moving portrait of a continuous action, the scenes being envisaged now from a distance, now close up, now frontally, now from the side, with each of these separate pictures a part of a whole action extending over time. Such an imagination, that of a great narrator, could find no expression in the visual arts of any age before our own: it is the art of the cinema.[1] The imagination of Propertius is limited by the scope of the painter or sculptor; but everything goes to show that within this limit it was more liberally nourished by acquaintance with, and indeed knowledge of, painting and sculpture than that of any other Augustan poet, so much so indeed that the images of nature unmodified by a painter's skill make little appearance in his work. There are some, notably where he is describing features of his own *patria*, as in 4.1.123 (cf. above, p. 96), but they are comparatively few.

Time and time again, when Propertius sees most vividly, he sees not the actual and contemporary in itself, but the ideal and sharp pictorial representation of something like. When in 1.3 he comes on the sleeping Cynthia imagination presents her as the sleeping Ariadne beloved by ancient sculptors and painters, or as the Maenad sleeping exhausted on the grassy bank of a stream that we see in a painting in the Naples Museum. In the same poem he is himself the Argus intent on Io represented in the Casa di Livia on the Palatine and in other versions at Naples. When he dreams of Cynthia drowning (2.26), the details of the picture are prompted by representations of the drowning of Helle (below, pp. 166 ff.). When he speaks of Calypso sitting on the shore, her

[1] This most helpful analogy is that of the admirable authors of *Aestimanda* (Oxford, 1965), M. G. Balme and M. S. Warman.

hair uncombed (1.15.11 f.), it is relevant to recall that the *Seated Calypso* of the painter Nicias was probably to be seen in Rome itself (Pliny, *Nat.* 35.132). Apollo leaning on his gilded lyre (3.3.14) is a figure we can also see at Naples; another couplet of the same poem (31 f.), where Venus' doves dip their scarlet beaks in the basin filled with the water of Hippocrene would never have been misinterpreted if people had remembered the frequent mosaic representations of doves drinking from basins, the most exquisite that from Hadrian's villa in the Museo Capitolino. The gardens of Pompeii, ruinous as they are, still present us with the mosaic-encrusted grotto and the clay masks of Silenus of 3.3.27 ff. This same imagination he attributed to Arethusa with her vision of Ocnus and his ass, a detail in Polygnotus' great painting of the underworld and in its imitations, and of the bare-breasted Amazon queen (above, p. 143).

For narrative, as we saw (above, p. 134), this kind of imagination is less than ideal, and especially for the elegiac narrator, whose episodic technique demands a more expansive visualisation than he deploys. Even in lesser-scale compositions, it clogs the story of Hylas (1.20) with over-elaborate pictorial elements (above, p. 39), and it leaves the story of Antiope (3.15) sometimes puzzlingly detailed, sometimes disconcertingly brusque. For it is a defect sometimes of the imagination fed by pictorial representation to be content with a rather stenographic verbal cash-out of a scene, just because its pictorial equivalent is vividly present. So when Propertius says (3.15.37 f.):

> *puerique trahendam*
> *vinxerunt Dircen sub trucis ora bovis.*

The lads bound Dirce to be dragged along under the countenance of a savage ox,

we may feel that though this is all very well for those who have met the Toro Farnese and Pompeian paintings of Dirce's punishment, and who can therefore think in the appropriate gestures and emotions, for those who have not it is a fraction curt. We find in many Augustan poets an equivalent reliance, sometimes misplaced, on the emotional carrying power of an allusion to other poetical treatments of a theme; but in none of them do we find such a reliance on the carrying power of an allusion to painting. Where Propertius does successfully deploy in narrative the static suggestions of a pictorial imagination thus limited, as he does in 4.6, it seems almost as if he succeeds because he has been warned off the attempt at depicting movement by the triumph of a master of movement (above, pp. 135f.).

Yet there are areas where he could not have achieved the success he does if his imagination had been of a different kind: no character in ancient poetry is so persuasively inconsequential as an Arethusa intent on the pictorial, no dreams so persuasively inconsequential as those of 3.3 (above, p. 79) and of 2.26. The dealings of some editors with 2.26 may serve to show the usefulness of approaching Propertius without keeping one's eyes shut to painting. Here is the poem:

> Vidi te in somnis fracta, mea vita, carina
> Ionio lassas ducere rore manus,
> et quaecumque in me fueras mentita fateri,
> nec iam umore gravis tollere posse comas,
> qualem purpureis agitatam fluctibus Hellen, 5
> aurea quam molli tergore vexit ovis.
>
> Quam timui ne forte tuum mare nomen haberet,
> teque tua labens navita fleret aqua!
> quae tum ego Neptuno, quae tum cum Castore fratri,
> quae tibi suscepi, iam dea, Leucothoe! 10
>
> At tu vix primas attollens gurgite palmas
> saepe meum nomen iam peritura vocas.
> quod si forte tuos vidisset Glaucus ocellos,
> esses Ionii facta puella maris,
> et tibi ob invidiam Nereides increpitarent, 15
> candida Nesaee, caerula Cymothoe.
>
> Sed tibi subsidio delphinum currere vidi,
> qui, puto, Arioniam vexerat ante lyram.
> iamque ego conabar summo me mittere saxo,
> cum mihi discussit talia visa metus. 20

1–6. I saw you in sleep, your ship wrecked, my life, trailing your weary hands in the Ionian sea, and confessing all your lies against me, and no longer able to hold up the weight of your drenched hair, like Helle tossed by purple waves, she whom the golden sheep carried on its soft fleece.

7–10. How afraid I was a sea might bear your name, and the sailor bewail you as he glides over your waters! What vows I undertook to Neptune, to Castor and his brother, and to you, now a goddess, Leucothoe![1]

11–16. But you, scarce uplifting your palms above the flood, kept calling my name as death was near. If Glaucus had chanced to see your eyes, you would have been made the girl of the Ionian sea, and the Nereids would be jealously carping at you, white Nesaee, blue Cymothoe.

17–20. But I saw a dolphin speeding to rescue you, the one, I fancy, that carried Arion and his lyre. And I was already trying to fling myself from the crag's top, when fear dispelled these visions.

The elements of this picture derive from representations of the drowning of Helle, of which Propertius has kept the central figure and the background, while deleting her brother Phrixus and demoting the ram with the golden fleece; in the works of art Phrixus is seated on the ram, and in some he stretches his arm down to try to grasp his sister's hand, thus providing the same motif of rescue that Propertius develops. The drenched hair that makes it all but impossible for Cynthia to keep her head above water, the hands outstretched in appeal, the speeding dolphin, the crags like that from which Propertius wishes to fling himself are all present in a mosaic in Naples. Propertius is quite conscious of deriving his scene from a picture and therefore offers the simile in the third couplet, underlining its pictorial character by the colour contrast between the purple waves and the golden fleece; the later contrast between *candida Nesaee* and *caerula Cymothoe* makes the same point.

Awareness of the derivation makes it possible for us to say that those editors who have wished to delete the simile of Helle are wrong, and so are those who have wished to put it after line 8 and attach it not to the opening description, but to the sentence 'How

---

[1] The divinised Ino, the cruel stepmother who persecuted Helle.

afraid I was . . .', and so are those who want not only Cymothoe but Nesaee to be blue. But we can go a good deal further than that. The principal plaint that editors have made against the poem concerns its logic: why, they ask, should Propertius wish to fling himself from the crag when he has already seen the dolphin speeding to the rescue? Suggested remedies are multiple: some remove the dolphin couplet altogether, some put after it the couplet beginning 'But you, scarce uplifting . . .', so as to show Cynthia once more in extremity and thus motivate Propertius' impetuous attempt at rescue, some retain the manuscript order and suggest that Propertius is jealous of the dolphin and therefore tries to save Cynthia himself.[1] To all this there is, of course, one sufficient answer: to hunt thus for some coherence, however unlikely, is to criticise not the logic of Propertius but the lack of logic in dreams. Yet this answer, though sufficient, can be filled out a little more: it might, one would say, have been difficult for the poet to arrive at this dreamlike inconsequence except by way of the apprehension of a painting; the poem's order of development, that is, seems to be dictated by the order of perception. When we look at the paintings of the drowning of Helle, our attention is first concentrated on her as the central and the powerfully emotional figure; the dolphin, to which Propertius gives a function, is in the pictorial representations merely a decorative element in the seascape, while the cliffs like that on which Propertius stands frame the seascape and are the last thing we come to attend to. In such a case the particular disconnectedness that comes from the concentration on an instant and isolated image, from the fragmented perception even of a single work of art, is turned to a unique advantage; and in such a case we shall not really comprehend much of what Propertius has to say unless we are willing to turn our eyes away from words and look more attentively than we have done at the monuments of art.

It is not all the famous sons of his Umbria that Propertius

---

[1] The author of this last notion prefixed to it the condition, 'If one wants logical coherence at all costs . . .'; and well he might. But it has been solemnly received: '*Quae interpretatio cum mihi probabilis videatur* . . .', 'There may be something in these latter thoughts . . .' and so on.

would have found congenial: the destiny that raised Marius and Cicero from one town, and Juvenal and St. Thomas from another, was similarly sportive when she endowed Assisi with Propertius and St. Francis, not to mention Santa Chiara, now patroness of television. But the achievement of Raphael, accurate, life-loving, allusive like his own, is one that Propertius would have been better placed than most Roman poets to comprehend.

Bibliography

GENERAL

The English reader has two commentaries available to him, that of H. E. Butler and E. A. Barber (Oxford, 1933) and that of W. A. Camps (Cambridge, published in four separate books from 1961 to 1967); neither are as complete as Max Rothstein's German commentary (ed. 2, Berlin, 1920, reprinted Dublin/Zürich, 1966). There are useful separate editions (in Latin) of Books I and II by P. J. Enk (Leiden, 1946 and 1962), of Book IV (in Italian) by Paolo Fedeli (Bari, 1965). Better in some discussions than any commentary is D. R. Shackleton Bailey's *Propertiana* (Cambridge, 1956); probably no one owes a deeper debt to this book (and to E. A. Barber's Oxford Classical Text, which appeared in 1953) than those of us who, in the Oxford manner of twenty years ago, have struggled to elucidate Phillimore's old OCT by the light of Butler and Barber's commentary, but anyone who cares about Latin poetry can learn much from it. A. E. Housman's numerous dealings with Propertius are now available in his *Collected Papers* (Cambridge, 1972). It is a pity that no publisher is likely to facilitate the labours of Propertian scholars by making a similar collection of the Propertian papers of J. P. Postgate and Arthur Palmer.

There are some recent books on Augustan poetry that no student of Propertius can afford to neglect, notably S. Lilja, *The Roman Elegists' Attitude to Women* (Helsinki, 1965), J. K. Newman, *Augustus and the New Poetry* (Brussels, 1967), Gordon Williams, *Tradition and Originality in Roman Poetry* (Oxford, 1968), Francis Cairns, *Generic Composition in Greek and Roman Poetry* (Edinburgh, 1972). On Propertius himself no English book is so comprehensive and sympathetic as A. La Penna, *Properzio* (Florence, 1951) or J.-P. Boucher, *Études sur Properce* (Paris, 1965), no examination of his manners of writing so thorough and discerning as Hermann Tränkle, *Die Sprachkunst des Properz und die Tradition der lateinischen Dichtersprache* (Wiesbaden, 1960).

CHAPTER ONE: THE MONOBIBLOS

For the development of Roman elegy, the most significant contribution is still Jacoby's magisterial article *Zur Entstehung der römischen Elegie*, *RhM* 60, 1905, 38 ff. (= *Kleine philologische Schriften* 2 [Berlin, 1961], pp. 65 ff.). Before Jacoby, literary historians assumed the existence of a Hellenistic personal elegy, from which that of Rome was directly derived and which was formally similar to it; he pointed out that this was contradicted by all we knew of the development of Hellenistic poetry, and that no single fragment could plausibly be assigned to such a personal elegy. Sixty-nine years later, after large increases in our knowledge of Hellenistic literature, this is still basically the case. The arguable exceptions are few and insufficient to controvert Jacoby's position: the poem of Poseidippus on old age (see Hugh Lloyd-Jones, *JHS* 83, 1963, 75 ff.) is in tone totally unlike any Roman elegy, the fragment of Parthenius' *Arete* (above, p. 10) comes from a poem that we can be pretty certain was formally quite unlike Roman elegy. Jacoby's position was tacitly accepted by Wilamowitz in *Sappho und Simonides* (Berlin, 1913) and in the second edition of *Hellenistische Dichtung* (Berlin, 1924), both of which are fundamental to study of the subject. For the English reader, Jacoby's arguments were soberly stated and evaluated in the introduction to Butler and Barber's commentary. Subsequent attempts to hold an impossible balance between Jacoby and pre-Jacoby theses (for example, in G. Luck's *The Latin Love Elegy* [London, 1959]) emphasise the strength of Jacoby's case.

There is a useful discussion of Propertius' debt to Callimachus and an inevitably more speculative one of his relation to Philetas in J.-P. Boucher, op. cit. pp. 161 ff. See also the contributions of A. Rostagni and P. Boyancé in *L'Influence grecque sur la poésie latine de Catulle à Ovide* (Fondation Hardt, 2, 1953). For Parthenius, cf. R. Pfeiffer, 'A Fragment of Parthenios' Arete', *CQ* 37, 1943, 23 ff. (= *Ausgewählte Schriften* [Munich, 1960], pp. 133 ff.); this article is much more comprehensive and important than its modest title suggests.

The development of Hellenistic epigram is displayed, with admirable discussion of individual poets, in *The Greek Anthology: Hellenistic Epigrams*, edited by A. S. F. Gow and D. L. Page (Cambridge, 1965), that of late Republican and early imperial epigram in *The Greek Anthology: The Garland of Philip*, by the same editors (Cambridge, 1968); these considerable works unfortunately make no attempt to give an overall *mise-en-scène*. The subject is discussed in *L' Épigramme*

grecque (Fondation Hardt 14, 1967); for the student of Roman elegy
the most useful sections are G. Giangrande, *Sympotic Literature and
Epigram* and W. Ludwig, *Die Kunst der Variation im hellenistischen
Liebesepigramm.*
For what can be known and conjectured about Gallus, cf. J.-P.
Boucher, *Caius Cornelius Gallus* (Paris, 1966).

CHAPTER TWO: SOME PROBLEMS OF UNITY

For rather different analyses of 2.28, see U. Knoche, *Miscellanea
Properziana*, Atti dell' Accademia Properziana del Subasio (Assisi,
1957), pp. 49 ff.; R. E. White, *TAPhA* 89, 1958, 245 ff.
On the relation of Propertius to Tibullus, cf. S. d'Elia, *RAAN* 28,
1954, 1 ff.; Enk, Book II pp. 34 ff. I disagree profoundly with the
conclusion they concur in, 'that the points of contact, though interesting, are purely superficial.'

CHAPTER THREE: THE QUEST FOR CALLIMACHUS

The dedication of the poet on Helicon and its associated imagery are
thoroughly explored in A. Kambylis, *Die Dichterweihe und ihre
Symbolik* (Heidelberg, 1965); cf. also O. Skutsch, *Studia Enniana*
(London, 1968), pp. 1–29, 119–29, J.-P. Boucher, *Études*, pp. 173 ff.
For the influence of Horace's *Odes* on Book III, see F. Solmsen,
CPh 43, 1948, 105 ff.; D. Flach, *Das literarische Verhältnis von Horaz
und Properz*, Giessen, 1967.
Sir Ronald Syme's *The Roman Revolution* (Oxford, 1939) is of
course fundamental to the understanding of the age in which the
elegists wrote; Chapters XXIX and XXX are particularly relevant.
For Propertius' attitude to society and politics cf. Boucher, *Études*,
Chapters I and V.
The ease, *otium*, prized by the elegists is a concept with a rich and
complicated history, examined in J.-M. André, *L'Otium dans la vie
morale et intellectuelle romaine* (Paris, 1966); cf. especially Chapter VII.
The elegists' definition of *otium* is partial and persuasive, their defence
of it anti-traditional, in a way that is clarified by other defences of a
different *otium*; D. C. Earl, *The Political Thought of Sallust* (Cambridge,
1961) is useful here.
Omission can sometimes be instructive: J. Béranger, *Recherches sur
l'aspect idéologique du principat* (Basle, 1953), a careful examination of

the favoured encomiastic terminology of the principate, has no mention of Propertius.

CHAPTER FOUR: PROPERTIUS' LAST BOOK

The article of G. P. Goold, '*Noctes Propertianae*', *HSCPh* 71, 1966, 59 ff., though valuable to anyone considering any part of Propertius, is particularly relevant to Book IV.

CHAPTER FIVE: RETROSPECT

On allusiveness in Propertius' imagery in Book III, see W. R. Smyth, *CQ* 43, 1949, 122 f.

There are good pages on the artistic sensibility of Propertius in Boucher, *Études*, pp. 41 ff., and a further bibliography there.

Cuts of pictures and further references to them can be found in S. Reinach, *Répertoire des peintures grecques et romaines* (Paris, 1922) and in W. H. Roscher, *Ausführliches Lexikon der griechischen und römischen Mythologie* (Leipzig, 1884–1937). A few can be seen more accessibly and attractively represented in Amadeo Maiuri, *Roman Painting* (Lausanne, 1953) and in E. Pfuhl, *Masterpieces of Greek Drawing and Painting* (London, 1955). The following references do not aim to be more than helpful, and to choose, where there is a choice, the more attractive representation:

Apollo leaning on his lyre (3.3.14): Maiuri, p. 85.

Argus and Io (1.3.19 f.): Maiuri, p. 26.

Ariadne (1.3.1 f.): Reinach 113.1, 2 (paintings), Roscher 1.545 (sculpture).

Boreas and Orithyia (1.20.29 f.): Roscher 1.1.807.

Dirce's punishment (3.15.37 f.): Reinach 184.2, 185.1, 2, 4.

Doves drinking (3.3.31 f.): Pfuhl, pl. 155 (the doves of the Museo Capitolino), Maiuri, p. 128 (a good photograph of a much inferior mosaic).

Helle drowning (2.26): Roscher 3.2.2466.

Hylas' fountain (1.20.33 ff.): Roscher 1.2.2795.

Maenad sleeping (1.3.5 f.): prettily reproduced in W. Dräyer and K. Schefold, *Pompeji: Zeugnisse griechischer Malerei* (Munich, 1956), pl. 6.

Ocnus and his ass (4.3.21 f.): Roscher 3.1.822 f.

Index of Poems and Passages

General Index

Academy, 90 n.1
Acanthis, 137 ff.
Achilles, 108, 149 f., 152
Acontius, 11, 33
Acron, 130
Actium, 40, 43, 60, 62, 98, 108, 111, 113, 134 ff.
address to the absent, 33
Aemilia, 148
Aemilius Paullus, L., 79 n.2
Aeneas, 38
Aetia: of Callimachus, 10 ff., 73 f., 80, 118 f.; projected by Propertius, 114 ff., 156
aetiology, 118 ff.
Afranius, 68 f.
Aganippe, 74 f.
Agathias, 14
Agrippa, 117, 135
Alba Longa, kings of, 79
Alcinous, 78
Alexandria, 84, 94
Alfenus Varus, 99
Allius, 12
Alcaeus, 69
Alphesiboea, 30 f., 54 n.1
Amphion, 77, 165
Anacreon, 20, 102 n.2
André, J.-M., 172
Andromache, 56 n.1, 101 n.1, 150
Andromeda, 21, 49, 54 n.1, 151
Anna Perenna, 125
Antilochus, 150
Antimachus, 10
Antinous, 142
Antiope, 165
Antonius, L., 97
Antonius, M., 61 f., 102 n.1, 112 f., 136
Aphthonius, 23

Apollo: and Actium, 135 f.; and Callimachus, 73 ff., 99, 159; and Gallus, 75; and Propertius, 46, 77 ff.; and pseudonyms, 12; and the *cithara*, 102, 165, 173; and the Palatine temple, 43 f., 102 f., 134 f.
Apollonius Rhodius, 37, 70
apology, Callimachean (*recusatio*), 70, 99 ff., 109 ff.
Arabia, 43
Archias, 11
Archilochus, 69
Archytas, 86
Arētē, 10, 171
Arethusa, 142 ff., 163, 165
Argonauts, 37 f.
Argus, 21, 164, 173
Ariadne, 21, 33, 128, 164, 173
Aristotle, 7, 10, 28 n.1, 51, 153
Arnobius, 121
art, visual, 21, 38, 80, 90 n.1, 109, 143, 164 ff., 173
Artemis, 56
Ascanius, 37 f.
Assisi, vii, 96 f., 169
Atalanta, 16 f., 19, 38
Athens, 90
Atkinson, K. M. T., 42 f.
Augustan *régime*, 42, 93 ff.
Augustus, vii, 40, 42 ff., 60 n.2, 75, 89, 97 ff., 117, 131, 135 f., 147 f.

Bacchus, 72, 75, 79, 81, 89
Bacchylides, 78
Baehrens, E., 34 n.2
Bailey, D. R. Shackleton, 170
Balme, M. G., 164 n.1
Barber, E. A., 41, 44, 170 f.
Barrett, W. S., 26 n.1